THE LIGHT BEYOND

Other books by Raymond Moody

LIFE AFTER LIFE
REFLECTIONS ON LIFE AFTER LIFE

THE LIGHT BEYOND

RAYMOND A. MOODY, JR., M.D.

with Paul Perry

Foreword by Andrew Greeley

BANTAM BOOKS
TORONTO · NEW YORK · LONDON · SYDNEY · AUCKLAND

Grateful acknowledgment is made for permission to reprint the following excerpts:

Page 16–19 Reprinted with permission from James H. Lindley, Sethyn Bryan, & Bob Conley, Near-death experiences in a Pacific Northwest American population: The Evergreen study. ANABIOSIS: THE JOURNAL OF NEAR-DEATH STUDIES, 1981, 1, 104–124.

Page 20–21 Reprinted with permission from Kenneth Ring, Precognitive amd prophetic visions in near-death experiences. ANABIOSIS: THE JOURNAL OF NEAR-DEATH STUDIES, 1982, 2, 47–74.

Page 144–45 Reprinted with permission from J. Timothy Green & Penelope Friedman, Near-death experiences in a Southern California population. ANABIOSIS: THE JOURNAL OF NEAR-DEATH STUDIES, 1983, 3, 77–95.

Page 122–127 Reprinted by permission of Putnam Publishing Group, LIFE AT DEATH by Kenneth Ring copyright © 1980 by Kenneth Ring. British rights made by permission of the author.

THE LIGHT BEYOND
A Bantam Book / August 1988

Library of Congress Cataloging-in-Publication Data

Moody, Raymond A.
  The light beyond.

  Bibliography: p. 157
  1. Near-death experiences. I. Perry, Paul,
1950–   . II. Title.
BL535.M65   1988   133.9'01'3   88-6388
ISBN 0-553-05285-3

Published simultaneously in the United States and Canada

Bantam Books are published by Bantam Books, a division of Bantam Doubleday Dell Publishing Group, Inc. Its trademark, consisting of the words "Bantam Books" and the portrayal of a rooster, is Registered in U.S. Patent and Trademark Office and in other countries. Marca Registrada. Bantam Books, 666 Fifth Avenue, New York, New York 10103.

PRINTED IN THE UNITED STATES OF AMERICA

DH   0 9 8 7 6 5 4 3 2 1

CONTENTS

Foreword

Raymond Moody has achieved a rare feat in the quest for human knowledge: he has created a paradigm.

In his classic *The Structure of Scientific Revolutions*, Thomas Kuhn points out that scientific revolutions occur when someone creates a new perspective, a new model, a new approach to reality. After such a breakthrough, great progress can be made that was previously impossible. Scientific progress, Kuhn contends, is less the result of the dogged work of applying the scientific method to problems and more the result of a brilliant and original insight that opens the way for such work.

As Dr. Moody notes in the present volume, *Life After Life* is not the first book about such experiences. Indeed, Dr. Carol Zaleski of Harvard, in her fascinating study, *Otherworld Journeys*, tells us that the literature of the Middle Ages is filled with similar accounts. Moody did not, then, discover these experiences. But he put a name to them, and that name, NDE—near-death experiences—provided the paradigm for the considerable research that has occurred since the publication of *Life After Life*.

Why is giving a phenomenon the right name so important? Stephen Hawking, the great English theoretical physicist, has said that the name *black hole* for the phenomenon he is studying is of critical importance. So in every human activity, since we are naming creatures—creatures who bestow meaning on phenomena—the names we choose determine how we explain the phenomena and what others do with our work.

Not only did Dr. Moody rediscover an experience that, as we now know, is widespread in the human condition, but he also, by assigning that experience the precisely appropriate label, assured that there would be more research and study of the experience. It is impossible to overestimate the importance of such a contribution to human knowledge.

The Light Beyond, like Dr. Moody's previous efforts, is characterized by openness, sensitivity, and modesty. The last characteristic is, I think, the most important in his work. He makes no extreme claims for his findings. The very label *near-death experience* is so effective because it is so utterly modest. Dr. Moody does not claim that he has proved anything more than the existence and the widespread prevalence of the NDE.

Has the NDE research scientifically proved that there is life after death? I think not, despite some of the enthusiastic claims that have been made for it. It merely proves that at the time of death many people undergo a benign and promising experience. I don't think that on the subject of human survival anything more than that conclusion can be expected. Thus I fail to see why much of the scientific and medical establishments cannot be content with the demonstrated fact that these experiences occur and study them with interest and respect.

Does the NDE research increase the probabilities of human survival beyond death? I rather think it does; but, as long as one is working with probabilities, there is still required a leap of faith, which most of those who have had an NDE do not hesitate to make.

Near the end of this book, Dr. Moody turns to a man who was perhaps America's greatest thinker, William James. The NDE is a "noetic" experience, an experience of illumination that purports to provide understanding that is unassailable for one who has encountered it. As James himself remarks, such experiences cannot constrain acceptance from empirical science; but, since such experiences occur, empirical science cannot claim a monopoly on human ways of knowing. Carol Zaleski arrives at the same conclusion at the end of her investigation; as does Dr. Moody, she falls back on the categories of William James: the NDE is an experience of mystical illumination.

"Otherworld visions are products of the same imaginative power that is active in our ordinary ways of visualizing death; our tendency to portray ideas in concrete, embodied, and dramatic forms; the capacity of our inner states to transfigure our perception of outer landscapes; our need to internalize the cultural map of the physical universe; and our drive to experience that universe as a moral and spiritual cosmos in which we belong and have a purpose."

The NDE then is one of many hope renewal experiences that occur in human life—though a spectacular one. It is a hint of an explanation, though a powerful hint.

It is not the only hint.

Dr. Zaleski, in correspondence with me about her work, remarked that her letter had been delayed by the advent of her first child. I wrote back that I wondered if the birth of a child might not be at least as strong a hint of an explanation as an NDE, if a much more commonplace hint. From the perspective of the Ultimate, the question might well be whether He can give better hints or more hints than He already has.

Be that as it may, the hints, the rumors of angels, are not much use to those who are inclined to listen to them, unless they influence their lives. As Dr. Zaleski remarks, "A conviction that life surpasses death, however intensely felt, will eventually lose its vitality and become a mere fossil record, as alien as any borrowed doctrine, unless it is tested and rediscovered in daily life."

As I read Dr. Moody's exploration of light and Light, he seems to be making the same argument. The Light came into the darkness and the darkness could not put it out.

Andrew Greeley
Chicago
All Souls/Samain
1987

THE LIGHT BEYOND

CHAPTER 1

The Experience of Almost Dying

What happens when people die? That is probably mankind's most often asked and perplexing question. Do we simply cease to live, with nothing but our mortal remains to mark our time on earth? Are we resurrected later by a Supreme Being only if we have good marks in the Book of Life? Do we come back as animals, as the Hindus believe, or perhaps as different people generations later?

We are no closer to answering the basic question of the afterlife now than we were thousands of years ago when it was first pondered by ancient man. But there are many ordinary people who have been to the brink of death and reported miraculous glimpses of a world beyond, a world that glows with love and understanding that can be reached only by an exciting trip through a tunnel or passageway.

This world is attended by deceased relatives bathed in glorious light and ruled by a Supreme Being who guides the new arrival through a review of his life before sending him back to live longer on earth.

Upon return, the persons who "died" are never the same. They embrace life to its fullest and express the belief that love and knowledge are the most important of all things because they are the only things you can take with you.

For want of a better phrase to describe these incidents, we can say these people have had near-death experiences (NDEs).

I coined this phrase several years ago in my first book, *Life After Life*. Other people have called it other things, including "otherworld journeys," "flight of the alone to the Alone," "breaking of the plane," "near-death visions." But the traits of these episodes—no matter what they are called—all point to a similar experience. NDEers experience some or all of the following events: a sense of being dead, peace and painlessness even during a "painful" experience, bodily separation, entering a dark region or tunnel, rising rapidly into the heavens, meeting deceased friends and relatives who are bathed in light, encountering a Supreme Being, reviewing one's life, and feeling reluctance to return to the world of the living.

I isolated these traits over two decades ago in personal research that started by coincidence when I was a twenty-year-old philosophy student at the University of Virginia.

I was sitting with a dozen or so students in a seminar room listening to Professor John Marshall discuss the philosophical issues related to death. Marshall mentioned that he knew a psychiatrist in town—Dr. George Ritchie—who had been pronounced dead of double pneumonia and then successfully resuscitated. While he was "dead," Ritchie had the remarkable experience of passing through a tunnel and seeing beings of light.

This experience, my professor remarked, had profoundly affected this physician, who was convinced that he had been allowed to peek into the afterlife.

Frankly, at that point in my life, the prospect that we

might survive spiritually after physical death had never occurred to me. I had always assumed that death was an obliteration of one's physical body as well as one's consciousness. Naturally I was intrigued that a respected physician would be confident enough to publicly admit having a glimpse of the afterlife.

A few months later I heard the psychiatrist himself describe his experience to a group of students. He told us of viewing from a distance his own apparently dead body as it lay on a hospital bed, of entering into a brilliant light that emanated love, and of seeing every event of his life reviewed in a three-dimensional panorama.

I filed Ritchie's story away in my memory and went on with my studies, finishing my Ph.D. in philosophy in 1969. It was when I began teaching at the university that I ran into another near-death experience.

One of my students had almost died the year before, and I asked him what the experience was like. I was overwhelmed to find that he'd had an episode almost exactly like the one I had heard from Ritchie over four years before.

I began to find other students who knew of other NDEs. By the time I entered medical school in 1972, I had no fewer than eight NDE case studies from reliable, sincere people.

In medical school I found more cases and soon had enough case studies to compile *Life After Life*, which became an international best-seller. There was clearly a thirst for knowledge about what happens to us in the hereafter.

The book posed many questions it couldn't answer and raised the ire of skeptics who found the case studies of a few hundred people to be worthless in the realm of "real" scientific study. Many doctors claimed that they had never heard of near-death experiences despite having resuscitated hundreds of people. Others claimed it was simply a form of mental illness, like schizophrenia. Some said these NDEs only happened to extremely religious people, while others felt it was a form of demon possession. These experiences never happen to children, some doctors said, because they haven't been "culturally polluted" like adults. Too few people have NDEs for them to be significant, others said.

Some people were interested in researching the subject of NDEs further, myself included. The work we have done over the last decade has shed a tremendous amount of light on this subject. We have been able to address most of the questions put forth by those who feel that the near-death experience is little more than a mental illness or the brain playing tricks on itself.

Frankly, it has been good to have the skeptics around, because it has made us look at this phenomenon much harder than we probably would have otherwise. Much of what we researchers have found is included in this book.

Who, How Many, and Why

One thing I would like to discuss in this chapter is the great number of NDEs that actually happen. When I started looking into this phenomenon, I thought there were very few people who actually experienced it. I had no figures and there were certainly none referred to in medical literature, but if I had to guess I would say that one in eight people who were resuscitated or had a similar brush with mortality had at least one of the traits of an NDE.

When I began lecturing and asking large groups of people if they had ever had an NDE themselves or knew anyone who had, my perception of the frequency of this phenomenon changed dramatically. At lectures I would ask the audience, "How many of you have had a near-death experience or know of someone who has?" About one person in thirty raised his hand in reply.

Pollster George Gallup, Jr., found that eight million adults in the United States have had an NDE. That equals one person in twenty.

He was further able to analyze the content of these NDEs by polling for their elements. Here is what he found:

ELEMENT	PERCENT
Out of body	26
Accurate visual perception	23
Audible sounds or voices	17
Feelings of peace, painlessness	32
Light phenomena	14
Life review	32
Being in another world	32
Encountering other beings	23
Tunnel experience	9
Precognition	6

Such a poll clearly showed that NDEs are much more common in society than any of the NDE researchers ever thought.

The NDE Traits

As I mentioned earlier, I was able to derive a set of nine traits that define the near-death experience. I did this by questioning hundreds of people and examining their unique episodes for those common elements.

In *Life After Life* I said that I had never met anyone who had experienced all of these traits while undergoing an NDE.

But since writing that book, I have interviewed more than a thousand NDEers and have found several who had "full-blown" episodes that exhibited all nine NDE traits.

Still, it's important to note that not all people who undergo a near-death experience have all of the following symptoms. Some might have one or two, others five or six. It is the presence of one or more of these traits that define the NDE.

A Sense of Being Dead

Many people don't realize that the near-death experience they are having has anything to do with death. They will find themselves floating above their body, looking at it from a distance, and suddenly feel fear and/or confusion. They will wonder, "How is it that I can be up here, looking at myself down there?" It doesn't make any sense to them and they become very confused.

At this point, they may not actually recognize the physical body they are looking at as being their own.

One person told me that while he was out of his body, he passed through an army hospital ward and was amazed at how many young men there were who were about his age and shape who looked like him. He was actually looking at these different bodies, wondering which one was his.

Another person who was in a horrible accident in which he lost two of his limbs remembered lingering over his body on the operating table and feeling sorry for the maimed person on it. Then he realized it was him!

NDEers often feel fear at this point, which then gives way to perfect understanding of what is going on. They can understand what the doctors and nurses are trying to convey to each other (even though they frequently have no formal medical training), but when they try to talk to them or other people present, no one is able to see or hear them.

At this point, they may try to attract the attention of the people present by touching them. But when they do, their hands go right through the person's arm as though nothing was there.

This was described to me by a woman I personally resuscitated. I saw her have a cardiac arrest and immediately started chest massage. She told me later that while I was working on restarting her heart, she was going up above her body and looking down. She was standing behind me, trying to tell me to stop, that she was fine where she was. When I didn't hear her, she tried to grab my arm to keep me from inserting a needle in her arm for injecting intravenous fluid. Her hand passed right through my arm. But when she did that, she later claimed that she felt something that was the consistency of "very rarified gelatin" that seemed to have an electric current running through it.

I have heard similar descriptions from other patients.

After trying to communicate with others, NDEers frequently have an increased sense of self-identity. One NDEer described this stage as being "a time when you are not the wife of your husband, you are not the parent of your children, you are not the child of your parents. You are totally and completely you." Another woman said she felt like she was going through "a cutting of ribbons," like the freedom given to a balloon when its strings are cut.

It is at this point that fear turns to bliss, as well as understanding.

Peace and Painlessness

While the patient is in his or her body, there can frequently be intense pain. But when the "ribbons are cut," there is a very real sense of peace and painlessness.

I have talked to cardiac arrest patients who say that the

7

intense pain of their heart attack turns from agony to an almost intense pleasure. Some researchers have theorized that the brain, when it experiences such intense pain, releases a self-made chemical that stops the pain. I discuss this theory in Chapter 7, but I will say here that no one has ever done experiments to prove or disprove it. But even if it is true, it doesn't explain the other symptoms of this phenomenon.

Out-of-Body Experience

Frequently about the time that the doctor says, "We've lost him (or her)," the patient undergoes a complete change of perspective. He feels himself rising up and viewing his own body below.

Most people say they are not just some spot of consciousness when this happens. They still seem to be in some kind of body even though they are out of their physical bodies. They say the spiritual body has shape and form unlike our physical bodies. It has arms and a shape although most are at a loss to describe what it looks like. Some people describe it as a cloud of colors, or an energy field.

One NDEer I spoke to several years ago said he studied his hands while he was in this state and saw them to be composed of light with tiny structures in them. He could see the delicate whorls of his fingerprints and tubes of light up his arms.

The Tunnel Experience

The tunnel experience generally happens after bodily separation. I didn't notice until I wrote *Life After Life* that it isn't until people undergo the "cutting of the ribbons" and the out-of-body experience that they truly realize that their experience has something to do with death.

At this point, a portal or tunnel opens to them and they are propelled into darkness. They start going through this dark space and at the end they come into the brilliant light that we'll deal with next.

Some people go up stairways instead of through a tunnel. One woman said she was with her son as he was dying of lung cancer. One of the last things he said was that he saw a beautiful spiral staircase going upward. He put his mother's mind at peace when he told her that he thought he was going up those stairs.

Some people have described going through beautiful, ornate doors, which seems very symbolic of a passage into another realm.

Some people hear a *whoosh* as they go into the tunnel. Or they hear an electric vibrating sensation or a humming.

The tunnel experience is not something I discovered. There is a fifteenth-century painting by Hieronymus Bosch called "The Ascent into the Empyrean" that visually describes this experience. In the foreground are people who are dying. Surrounding them are spiritual beings who are trying to direct their attention upward. They pass through a dark tunnel and come out into a light. As they go into this light, they kneel reverently.

In one of the most amazing tunnel experiences I've ever heard the tunnel was described as being almost infinite in length and width and filled with light.

The descriptions are many, but the sense of what is happening remains the same: the person is going through a passageway toward an intense light.

People of Light

Once through the tunnel, the person usually meets beings of light. These beings aren't composed of ordinary light.

They glow with a beautiful and intense luminescence that seems to permeate everything and fill the person with love. In fact, one person who went through this experience said, "I could describe this as 'light' or 'love' and it would mean the same thing." Some say it's almost like being drenched by a rainstorm of light.

They also describe this light as being much brighter than anything we experience on earth. But still, despite its brilliant intensity, it doesn't hurt the eyes. Instead, it's warm, vibrant, and alive.

In this situation, NDEers frequently meet up with friends and relatives who have died. Often, they speak of these people as being in the same indescribable bodies as theirs.

Besides bright light and luminescent friends and relatives, some people have described beautiful pastoral scenes. One woman I know spoke of a meadow that was surrounded by plants, each with its own inner light.

Occasionally, people see beautiful cities of light that defy description in their grandeur.

In this state, communication doesn't take place in words as we know them, but in telepathic, nonverbal ways that result in immediate understanding.

The Being of Light

After meeting several beings in light, the NDEer usually meets a supreme Being of Light. People with a Christian background often describe Him as God or Jesus. Those with other religious backgrounds may call him Buddha or Allah. But some have said that it's neither God nor Jesus, but someone very holy nonetheless.

Whoever he is, the Being radiates total love and understanding. So much so, that most people want to be with it forever.

But they can't. At this point they are told, usually by the Being of Light, that they have to return to their earthly body. But first it's his job to take them on a life review.

The Life Review

When the life review occurs, there are no more physical surroundings. In their place is a full color, three-dimensional, panoramic review of every single thing the NDEers have done in their lives.

This usually takes place in a third-person perspective and doesn't occur in time as we know it. The closest description I've heard of it is that the person's whole life is there at once.

In this situation, you not only see every action that you have ever done, but you also perceive immediately the effects of every single one of your actions upon the people in your life.

So for instance, if I see myself doing an unloving act, then immediately I am in the consciousness of the person I did that act to, so that I feel their sadness, hurt, and regret.

On the other hand, if I do a loving act to someone, then I am immediately in their place and I can feel the kind and happy feelings.

Through all of this, the Being is with those people, asking them what good they have done with their lives. He helps them through this review and helps them put all the events of their life in perspective.

All of the people who go through this come away believing that the most important thing in their life is love.

For most of them, the second most important thing in life is knowledge. As they see life scenes in which they are learning things, the Being points out that one of the things they can take with them at death is knowledge. The other is love.

When people come back they have a thirst for knowledge. Frequently, NDEers become avid readers, even if they weren't very fond of books before, or they enroll in school to study a different field than the one they are in.

Rising Rapidly into the Heavens

I should point out that not all NDEers have a tunnel experience. Some report a "floating experience," in which they rise rapidly into the heavens, seeing the universe from a perspective reserved for satellites and astronauts.

The psychotherapist C. G. Jung had an experience like this in 1944 when he had a heart attack. He said that he felt himself rise rapidly to a point far above the earth.

One child I talked to said that he felt himself rise far above the earth, passing through the stars and finding himself up with the angels. Another NDEer described himself as zooming up and seeing the planets all around him and the earth below like a blue marble.

Reluctance to Return

For many people, the NDE is such a pleasant event that they don't want to return. As a result, they are frequently very angry at their doctors for bringing them back.

Two physician friends of mine first discovered NDEs for themselves when patients they saved became hostile.

One of them was resuscitating another physician who had just had a cardiac arrest. When the stricken man revived, he said angrily: "Carl, don't you ever do that to me again."

Carl was bewildered as to why this anger should arise. But later the revived physician took him aside and apologized for his behavior and explained his experience. "I was mad because you brought me back to death instead of life."

Another physician friend of mine discovered the NDE phenomenon when he resuscitated a man who then yelled at him for taking him out of "that beautiful and bright place."

NDEers frequently act this way. But it is a short-lived feeling. If you talk to them a week or so later, they are happy to have returned. Although they miss the blissful state, they are glad to have the chance to go on living.

Interestingly, many NDEers feel they are given a choice to return or stay. It may be the Being of Light who offers this choice to them, or a relative who has died.

All of the persons I have talked to would stay if they had only themselves to think of. But they usually say they want to go back because they have children left to raise or because their spouses or parents might miss them.

One woman in Los Angeles has faced this question from the Being of Light twice in her life. Once in the late fifties when she was in a coma following an automobile accident, the Being told her it was time to die and go to heaven.

She argued with him, complaining that she was too young to die. But the Being wouldn't budge until she said, "But I'm young, I haven't danced enough yet."

At that point the Being gave out a hearty laugh and allowed her to live.

About thirty years later, she had a cardiac arrest while undergoing minor surgery. Again she passed through the tunnel and found herself with the Being, and again he told her it was her time to die.

This time she argued that she had children to raise and couldn't leave them at this point in their lives.

"Okay," said the Being. "But this is the last time. The next time you have to stay."

Different Time and Space

In addition to these nine traits, people who have undergone NDEs say that time is greatly compressed and nothing like the time we keep with our watches. NDEers have described it as "being in eternity." One woman, when asked how long her experience lasted, told me, "You could say it lasted one second or that it lasted ten thousand years and it wouldn't make any difference how you put it."

The boundaries imposed by space in our everyday lives are often broken in NDEs. During the experience, if NDEers want to go somewhere, they can often just think themselves there. People say that while they were out of their body but watching the doctors work on them in the operating room, they could simply wish their way into the waiting room to see their relatives.

Such experiences are perhaps the best answer to people who think NDEs are the brain playing tricks on itself. After all, on the surface it is entirely possible that the brain, while in great distress, could try to calm itself by creating tunnel experiences and Beings of Light to put the person to rest. But NDEers who can tell you what was going on in other rooms while having their episodes are truly having out-of-body experiences.

I have several examples of people who had out-of-body experiences during their resuscitations and were able to leave the operating room to observe relatives in other parts of the hospital.

One woman who left her body went into the waiting room and saw that her daughter was wearing mismatched plaids.

What had happened was that the maid had brought the child to the hospital and in her haste had just grabbed the first two things off the laundry pile.

Later, when she told her family about her experience and

the fact that she had seen the girl in these mismatched clothes, they knew that she must have been in that waiting room with them.

Another woman had an out-of-body experience and left the room where her body was being resuscitated. From across the hospital lobby, she watched her brother-in-law as some business associate approached him and asked what he was doing in the hospital.

"Well, I was going out of town on a business trip," said the brother-in-law. "But it looks like June is going to kick the bucket, so I better stay around and be a pallbearer."

A few days later when she was recovering, the brother-in-law came to visit. She told him that she was in the room as he spoke to his friend, and erased any doubt by saying, "Next time I die, you go off on your business trip because I'll be just fine." He turned so pale that she thought he was about to have a near-death experience himself.

Another of these experiences happened to an elderly woman I was resuscitating. I was giving her closed heart massage on an emergency room examining table and the nurse assisting me ran into another room to get a vial of medication that we needed.

It was a glass-necked vial that you're supposed to hold in a paper towel while breaking off the top so you don't cut yourself. When the nurse returned, the neck was broken so I could use the medicine right away.

When the old woman came to, she looked very sweetly at the nurse and said, "Honey, I saw what you did in that room, and you're going to cut yourself doing that." The nurse was shocked. She admitted that in her haste to open the medicine, she had broken the glass neck with her bare fingers.

The woman told us that while we were resuscitating her, she had followed the nurse back to the room to watch what she was doing.

Some of the Research:
How Many, How Much?

As already mentioned, the Gallup polling organization found in a 1982 poll that eight million adult Americans had experienced NDEs. Since this amounts to roughly one person in twenty, researchers realized they would have no problem in finding NDEers to study. In fact, many such studies began before Gallup posed the life after life question to America.

One study, appropriately entitled "The Evergreen Study," was able to examine the near-death experiences of forty-nine residents of the northwestern United States.

These people were interviewed by the researchers (James Lindley, Sethyn Bryan, and Bob Conley of Evergreen State College in Olympia, Washington) using a standard method. First, the NDEers were allowed to give an uninterrupted account of their encounter with death. Then, after their narrative was completed, a series of standard questions about the experience were asked.

These questions were the same used by Kenneth Ring, a Connecticut psychologist who also examined the NDEs of dozens of people and published the results in an excellent book (*Life at Death: A Scientific Investigation of the Near-Death Experience,* 1980). His method of questioning NDEers has become the accepted method of discovering whether a person has had an NDE. His questions are neutral—up to a point—then gently probing.

The Evergreen researchers used the same questions in order to compare their results with those of Ring:

1. Was the kind of experience difficult to put into words? (If yes:) Can you try all the same to tell me why?

What was it about the experience that makes it so hard to communicate? Was it like a dream or different from a dream?

2. When this episode occurred, did you think you were dying or close to death? Did you actually think you were dead? Did you hear anyone actually say you were dead? What else do you recall hearing while in this state?

3. What were your feelings and sensations during the episode?

4. Did you hear any noises or unusual sounds during the episode?

5. Did you at any time feel as though you were traveling or moving? What was that experience like? (If appropriate:) Was this experience in any way associated with the noise (sound) you described before?

6. Did you at any time during this experience feel that you were somehow separate from your own physical body? During this time, were you ever aware of seeing your physical body? (Ask these questions in turn. Then, if appropriate, ask:) Could you describe this experience for me? How did you feel when you were in this state? When you were outside your own physical body, where were you? Did you have another body? (If yes:) Was there any kind of connection between yourself and your physical body? Any kind of link between the two that you could see? Describe it for me. When you were in this state, what were your perceptions of time? Of space? Of weight? Is there anything you could do while in this state that you could not do in your ordinary physical body? Were you aware of any tastes or odors? How, if at all, were your vision and hearing affected while in this state? Did you experience a sense of loneliness while in this state? How so?

7. During your episode, did you ever encounter other individuals, living or dead? (If affirmative:) Who were they? What happened when you met them? Did they

communicate to you? What? How? Why do you think they communicated what they did to you? How did you feel in their presence?

8. Did you at any time experience a light, glow, or illumination? Can you describe this to me? (If affirmative:) Did this "light" communicate anything to you? What? What did you make of this light? How did you feel? (Or how did it make you feel?) Did you encounter any religious figures such as angels, guardian spirits, Christ, and so forth? Did you encounter any frightening spirits such as demons, witches, or the devil?

9. When you were going through this experience, did your life—or scenes from your life—ever appear to you as mental images or memories? (If so:) Can you describe this to me further? What was this experience like? How did it make you feel? Did you feel you learned anything from this experience? If so, what?

10. Did you at any time have a sense of approaching some kind of boundary or limit or threshold or point of no return? (If so:) Can you describe this to me? Did you have any particular feelings or thoughts that you can recall as you approached this boundary? Do you have any idea what this boundary represented or meant?

11. (If patient has previously stated he or she came close to dying, ask:) When you felt close to dying, how did you feel? Did you want to come back to your body, to life? How did it feel when you did find yourself conscious again in your own body? Do you have any recollection of how you got back into your physical body? Do you have any idea why you didn't die at this time? Did you ever feel judged by some impersonal force?

12. This experience of yours has been recent, but I wonder if you feel it has changed you in any way. Do you think so or not? If it has changed you, in what way? (If necessary and appropriate, then ask:) Has this experience changed your attitude toward life? How? Has it altered

your religious beliefs? If so, how? Compared to how you felt before this experience, are you more or less afraid of death, or the same? (If appropriate:) Are you afraid of death at all? (If patient has attempted suicide, ask:) How has this experience affected your attitude toward suicide? How likely is it that you might try to commit suicide again? (Be tactful.)

13. (If this has not been fully covered in question 12, then ask, if patient has stated that he or she has come close to dying:) As one who has come close to dying, can you tell me, in your own way, what you now understand death to be? What does death now mean to you?

14. Is there anything else you'd like to add here concerning this experience or its effects on you?

By using the same questions as Ring, the Evergreen researchers were able to compare their results to the Connecticut researcher's larger study.

They divided the near-death experience into five broad stages rather than the nine specific ones I outlined above: Peace, Body Separation, Darkness, Light, and Inner Setting.

In the Evergreen study, 74.5 percent of the sample experienced the stage of peace during the NDE, whereas 60 percent experienced it in Ring's study.

The Evergreen researchers found accounts of this stage to be almost exhausting to listen to, since persons being interviewed often went on and on about the blissful peace and warmth they felt while in this state.

The stage of bodily separation was experienced by 70.9 percent of the Evergreen subjects and 37 percent of Ring's. Darkness, which could also be described as the tunnel experience, was found in 38.2 percent of the Evergreen NDEs and 23 percent of Ring's. Light, which could include beings of light, was encountered by 56.4 percent of the Evergreen NDEers and 16 percent of Ring's.

Inner Setting, described as paradise by many of the subjects, was experienced by 34.5 percent of the Evergreen subjects and 10 percent of Ring's.

Of all the people studied by the Evergreen researchers, there was only one "hellish" NDE, which they define as an NDE that contains extreme fear, panic, or anger and may also contain visions of demonic creatures. In that one, a man reported that he was ushered into hell by mistake during his second of three NDEs. His is an enlightening and entertaining interview:

Respondent: The second experience was different, I went downstairs! Downstairs was dark, people were howling, [there was] fire, they wanted a drink of water. . . . Then somebody came to me, I don't know who it was, he pushed me aside and said, "You're not coming down here. You're going back upstairs."

Interviewer: Did he actually use those words?

Respondent: Yeah. "You're going back upstairs. We don't want you down here because you're not mean enough."

Interviewer: Did you first experience the blackness and then . . .

Respondent: Pitch black. First we went down . . . it was pitch black.

Interviewer: Did you go down a tunnel?

Respondent: It was not a tunnel, more than a tunnel, a great big one. I was floating down. . . . There was a man there waiting, he says, "He's not the one."

Interviewer: Could you see the people that were yelling?

Respondent: I seen a lot of people down there, screaming, howling . . .

Interviewer: Were they also in clothes?

Respondent: No, no, no. No clothes at all.

Interviewer: They were nude?

Respondent: Yeah.

Interviewer: And there were how many, would you guess?

Respondent: Oh, Christ, you can't count them.
Interviewer: Thousands?
Respondent: I'd say about, almost a million to me.
Interviewer: Oh really? And they were all really miserable?
Respondent: They were miserable and hateful. They were asking me for water. They didn't have water.
Interviewer: And there was a presence that was watching over them?
Respondent: Yes, he was there. He had his little horns on . . .
Interviewer: He had horns on! Do . . . who do you think . . . do you recognize this person?
Respondent: Oh yes. I know him anywhere.
Interviewer: Who was it?
Respondent: The devil himself!

Experiences like these are rare ones. The Evergreen researchers combined their research with mine and Ring's and found that only 0.3 percent described their NDEs as being "hellish."

But one thing that isn't rare with an NDE is its tendency to change the person who has it. NDEs are such powerful instruments of change that many people have to undergo psychological therapy to figure out how to fit them into their lives.

On the whole, the NDE changes the person for the positive. But even a positive change can be difficult to cope with, if for no other reason than it's a sudden change. In addition, there are the emotional effects of seeing a better world and having to live in this one.

Perhaps one of the best examples of how an NDE can affect someone comes from writer Katherine Anne Porter, who had an NDE during a near fatal bout with influenza in 1918. As the author of *Ship of Fools* said in an interview:

I had seen my heavenly vision and the world was pretty dull after that. My mood for several years thereafter was that it was not a world worth living in. And yet one has faith, one has the inner core of strength that comes from somewhere, probably inherited from someone. Throughout my life there have been times during the day when I have both an intense wish to die and later an eagerness that can't wait to see the next day. In fact, if I hadn't been tough as an alley cat, I wouldn't be here today.

The Flashforward

For some, the NDE provides a glimpse into the future. This happens in such an extremely small percentage of NDEs that I'm reluctant to consider it one of the traits of an NDE. But it does nonetheless happen.

I discovered this for myself by accident. The year was 1975, several months before the publication of *Life After Life*. It was Halloween and my wife at the time, Louise, had taken our children out trick-or-treating.

They arrived at one house and were greeted by a pleasant man and woman who began to talk to the children. They asked the children their names and when my oldest said, "Raymond Avery Moody, the third," the woman looked startled.

"I must talk to your husband," she said to Louise.

When I spoke to this woman later on, she told me about her NDE in 1971. She'd had heart failure and lung collapse during surgery and had been clinically dead for a long time. During this experience, she met a guide who took her through a life review and gave her information about the future. Toward the end of the experience, she was shown a picture of me, given my full name, and told that "when the time was right," she would tell me her story.

I found this encounter remarkable. But even more remarkable are some of the flashforwards that Kenneth Ring has discovered in his research on this subject.

Although the number of cases in Ring's sample is so small that he can't offer any statistical analysis, he was able to find several examples of the phenomenon through the community of near-death researchers. In these cases, the NDEer has a vision of the future, generally during a deep NDE. Sometimes this information stays with a person immediately after the NDE. But other times, it comes back later, accompanied by a powerful sense of deja vu, that feeling that an event has already been experienced.

One such example of a flashforward from Ring's work comes from a man now living in the United States, but who was born and raised in England. At the age of ten, he had an NDE during emergency surgery for a burst appendix. In a letter to Ring, he wrote:

> After the operation, when convalescing, I was aware that there were some strange memories—and that's what they were—concerning events in my future life. I do not know how they got there . . . they were just there. . . . However, at that time [1941], and indeed until 1968, I simply did not believe them.

He then described five specific memories, including the age and circumstances of his death, which I won't quote here. Here are the first two of those memories:

> 1. You will be married at age twenty-eight.
> This was the first of the memories, and this was perceived as a flat statement—there was no emotion attached to it. . . .
> And this did indeed happen, even though at my twenty-eighth birthday I had yet to meet the person that I was to marry.
> 2. You will have two children and live in the house that you see.

By contrast to the first prediction, this was felt; perhaps experienced is the correct term. I had a vivid memory of sitting in a chair, from which I could see two children playing on the floor in front of me. And I knew that I was married, although in this vision there was no indication of who it was that I was married to. Now a married person knows what it's like to be married because he or she is married. But it is not possible for a single person to know what it feels like to be married; in particular, it is not possible for a ten-year-old boy to know what it feels like to be married! It is this strange, impossible feeling that I remember so clearly, and why this incident remained in my mind. I had a memory of something that was not to happen for almost twenty-five years hence! But it was not seeing the future, in the conventional sense, it was experiencing the future. In this incident the future was now.

In this "experience" I saw directly in front of me, and to the right as indicated. I could not see to the left, but I did know that the person that I was married to was sitting on that side of the room. The children playing on the floor were about four and three years old, the older one had dark hair, and was a girl; the younger one had fair hair, although it was a boy. But as it turns out, they are both girls. And I was also aware that behind the wall . . . there was something very strange that I did not understand at all. My conscious mind could not grasp it, but I just knew that something different was there.

This "memory" suddenly became present one day in 1968, when I was sitting in a chair, reading a book, and happened to glance over at the children. . . . I realized that this was the "memory" from 1941. After that I began to realize that there was something to these strange recollections. And the strange object behind the wall was a forced-air heater. These heating units were not—and to the best of my knowledge, are still not—used in England. This was why I could not grasp what it was; it was not in my sphere of knowledge in 1941.

As science struggles to get a handle on near-death experiences, it can not even begin to grasp flashforwards during NDEs. On a highly speculative level, Ring attempts to do so by implying the existence of a fourth dimension. In this dimension, NDEers can see their life like an overview of a range of mountains—in some cases from beginning to end. They can't change it. They can just "see" it.

CHAPTER 2

Changed Lives:
The Transforming Power of
Near-Death Experiences

There is one common element in all near-death experiences: they transform the people who have them. In my twenty years of intense exposure to NDEers, I have yet to find one who hasn't had a very deep and positive transformation as a result of his experience.

I don't mean to imply that an NDE turns persons into syrupy, uncritical Pollyannas. Although it certainly makes them more positive and pleasant to be around (especially if they weren't that pleasant before the near-death experience), it also leads to an active engagement with the real world. It helps them grapple with the unpleasant aspects of reality in an unemotional and clear-thinking way—a way that is new to them.

All of the scholars and clinicians I have talked to who have interviewed NDEers have come to the same conclusion: they are better people because of their experience.

Although NDEs are what is known in psychology as "crisis events," they don't have negative effects like some other crisis events might. For instance, a bad combat experience might leave a person "stuck" at that point in time. Many Vietnam veterans, for example, relive the horrifying scenes of death and destruction that they witnessed years ago in combat. They hallucinate to the point that they can smell the gunpowder and feel the tropical heat. This is a negative response to a crisis event.

Other traumatizing events like floods, tornadoes, fires, and automobile accidents can leave people overwhelmed and unable to put the event behind them. When that happens, they too are emotionally "stuck."

A near-death experience is as much a crisis event as combat, a car wreck, or a natural disaster. Indeed, NDEs are often caused by one of these. But rather than becoming emotionally stuck, NDEers respond in a one-sided way. The experience seems to demand that the person take some positive action in his life. Some say it is the peace that comes with feeling that there will be life after life. Others think it's their exposure to a higher being that has lead to a certain enlightenment.

One of my favorite pieces of research on the transformative powers of a NDE comes from Charles Flynn, a sociologist at Miami University in Ohio.

He examined data in twenty-one questionnaires that were administered by Kenneth Ring, the noted NDE researcher, to see specifically what changes were made by NDEers.

He found that the NDEers above all else have more concern for others than before the experience. They also have an increased belief in the afterlife and a greatly decreased fear of death.

Flynn's findings are very hopeful. Research like this lets us know that the NDE—though jolting—is a positive experience.

Although we still don't know how these experiences affect the feelings of the millions of people who have had them about such issues as nuclear war and hunger, or even the ultimate effects on their marriages, we do know that the NDEer is good at heart.

My entire psychiatric practice is devoted to counseling patients who have had near-death experiences. Although their NDEs bring them face to face with a host of problems that most of us never encounter, they have all been changed for the better. As you can see from the following case studies, an NDE increases one's personal growth.

One of the most startling examples that I've seen of personal growth through an NDE was the case of a man I'll call Nick. He was a con artist and an outright criminal who had done everything from bilking widows to running drugs. Crime had provided a good life for Nick. He had nice cars, fine clothes, and new houses, and no problems with his conscience to annoy him.

Then his life changed. He was golfing on a cloudy day when a thunderstorm suddenly developed. Before he could get off the greens, he was struck by lightning and "killed."

He hovered above his body for a moment and then found himself speeding down a dark tunnel toward a spot of light. He emerged into a bright pastoral setting where he was greeted by relatives and other people who were "glowing like Coleman lanterns."

He met a being of light that he still haltingly describes as God, who graciously led him through a life review. He relived his entire life, not only seeing his actions in three dimensions, but seeing and feeling the effects of his actions on others.

That experience changed Nick. Later, while recovering in the hospital, he felt the full effect of his life review. With the being of light, he had been exposed to pure love. He felt that when he really died, he would have to undergo the life review again, a process that would be very uncomfortable if he failed to learn from his first life review.

"Now," says Nick, "I always live my life knowing that someday I'll have to go through another life review."

I won't tell you what he does now for a living, except to assure you that it's an honest and helpful profession.

Another person who was changed dramatically by an NDE was a man I'll call Mark. All of his life he was obsessed with money and social position. He had run a medical equipment business, showing more concern with the fast sale and the quick buck than with servicing the equipment after it was sold.

Then, in his mid-forties, he had a severe heart attack. During this experience, he was reunited with his grand-mother and many other relatives and exposed to their pure love.

After he was revived, his perspective on life totally changed. All of the things that had driven him before were now much lower on his list of priorities—far below family, friendships, and knowledge.

He told me that while he was "on the other side," he made an agreement with the being of light that he would never again focus so heavily on money, but would instead devote himself to being kind.

Ironically, this new attitude has led to greater profits. "I'm nicer to be around," he told me with a grin. "So people want to buy more from me."

Researchers who have interviewed large numbers of NDEers have confirmed the aftereffects of the near-death experience. Some have even alluded to the "luminous serenity" exuded by so many of these people. It is as though they have looked into the future and know that everything is going to be all right.

I have been able to isolate eight kinds of personal changes that take place in a person undergoing an NDE. These changes were present in all the NDEers I have talked to. It is the combination of these factors that makes up the luminous serenity present in so many NDEers.

No Fear of Dying

After the event, NDEers no longer fear death. This means different things to different people. For some, the primary fear is of the terrible pain that they imagine accompanies dying. Others worry about who will take care of their loved ones in their absence. Permanent cessation of consciousness is what frightens still others.

People who are controlling and authoritarian fear the loss of control over themselves and others that they think death will bring. Fear of hell's fire and damnation frightens many, while some are simply afraid of the unknown.

When NDEers say they have lost their fear of death, they most often mean that they no longer fear the obliteration of consciousness or self. That isn't to say that they want to die anytime soon. What they say is that the experience makes life richer and fuller than ever before. The ones I know want more than ever to continue living. In fact, many feel they are living for the first time.

As one person put it:

For the first fifty-six years of my life, I lived in constant fear of death. My focus was on avoiding death, which I regarded as a terrible thing. After my experience, I realized that by living my entire life in fear of death, I was blocking my appreciation of life.

Fear of hellish punishment for earthly deeds is no longer a problem for many. When they see the review of their life, NDEers realize that the being of light loves and cares for them. They realize that he is not judgmental, but rather he wants them to develop into better people. This helps them eliminate fear and focus instead on becoming loving people.

You have to understand that the being of light isn't telling them that they have to change. My summation, after hearing hundreds of these cases, is that the people change willingly because they are in the presence of the standard of goodness, which makes them want to change their behavior radically.

One NDEer I spoke to had been a minister of the fire and brimstone variety. It wasn't infrequent, he said, for him to tell his congregation that if they didn't believe the Bible in a certain way, they would be condemned to burn eternally.

When he went through his NDE, he said the being of light told him not to speak to his congregation like this anymore. But it was done in a nondemanding way. The being just implied that what he was doing was making the lives of his congregation miserable. When this preacher returned to the pulpit, he did so with a message of love, not fear.

Also, loss of control no longer scares people who were compulsive previous to their NDE. With many, the need for control stems from fear. But many people have told me that after their NDEs, they feel they can no longer live their life from fear. This is due in part because these people now believe in an afterlife. But it is also the result of this glimpse of happiness they have received. How can they stay fearful and unhappy after seeing ultimate bliss?

Although fear of death is diminished, the will to live isn't. Most of the NDEers that I have met are mentally healthier than before their experience. Despite their confidence about an afterlife, none are in a particular hurry to "cash in" their current existence. As one NDEer told me:

> This doesn't make you want to go out and get run over by a truck to get back over there. I still have a strong instinct to survive. This experience I had makes me see that the will to survive is an instinct.
> Soon after my cardiac arrests, I took a fall off the front steps of my home. As I went down I felt myself grasping desperately for something to catch on to. Even then I was thinking, "This is odd. You know where you are going if you die, how wonderful it will be." But still I felt that grasp of fear catching in my throat. The survival instinct. It doesn't go away when you have one of these experiences.

Sensing the Importance of Love

"Have you learned to love?" is a question faced in the course of the episode by almost all NDEers. Upon their return, almost all of them say that love is the most important thing in life. Many say it is why we are here. Most find it the hallmark of happiness and fulfillment, with other values paling beside it.

As you might guess, this revelation radically changes the value structure of most NDEers. Where they may have been bigoted, they now see each individual as a loved person. Where material wealth was the pinnacle of achievement, brotherly love now reigns. As one NDEer told me:

> You know, this experience has a hold on your everyday life, from then on. Walking down the street is a different experience entirely, believe you me. I used to walk down the street in my own little world, with my mind on a dozen different little problems. Now I walk down the street and I

feel I am in an ocean of humanity. Each person I see, I want to get to know, and I am certain that if I really knew them I would love them.

A man who works in the office with me asked why I always had a smile on my face. He didn't know about my experience, so I told him that because I almost died I was happy to be alive and let it pass. Someday, he'll find out for himself.

A Sense of Connection with All Things

NDEers return with a sense that everything in the universe is connected. This is a difficult concept for them to define, but most have a newfound respect for nature and the world around them.

An eloquent description of this feeling was given to me by a hard-driving, no-nonsense businessman who had an NDE during a cardiac arrest when he was sixty-two:

The first thing I saw when I awoke in the hospital was a flower, and I cried. Believe it or not, I had never really seen a flower until I came back from death. One big thing I learned when I died was that we are all part of one big, living universe. If we think we can hurt another person or another living thing without hurting ourselves, we are sadly mistaken. I look at a forest or a flower or a bird now, and say, "That is me, part of me." We are connected with all things and if we send love along those connections, then we are happy.

An Appreciation of Learning

NDEers also have newfound respect for knowledge. Some say that this was the result of reviewing their lives. The being of light told them that learning doesn't stop when you die; that knowledge is something you can take with you. Others describe an entire realm of the afterlife that is set aside for the passionate pursuit of knowledge.

One woman described this place as a big university, where people were involved in deep conversations about the world around them. Another man described this realm as a state of consciousness where whatever you want is available to you. If you think of something you want to learn about, it appears to you and *is there for you to learn.* He said it was almost as though information was available in bundles of thought.

This includes information of any kind. For instance, if I wanted to know what it was like to be the president of the United States, I would need only to wish for the experience and it would be so. Or if I wanted to know what it was like to be an insect, I would merely have to "request" the experience by wishing for it, and the experience would be mine.

This brief—albeit powerful—learning experience has changed the lives of many NDEers. The short time they were exposed to the possibility of total learning made them thirst for knowledge when they returned to their bodies.

Often, they embark on new careers or take up serious courses of study. None that I know of, however, have pursued knowledge for the sake of knowledge. Rather, they all feel that knowledge is important only if it contributes to the wholeness of the person. Once again, a sense of connectedness comes into play: knowledge is good if it helps make something whole.

The businessman quoted in the preceding section said it better than any researcher:

> *Doctor, I have to admit to you that before this cardiac arrest, I had only contempt for scholars. I worked my way up with little schooling, and I worked hard. There is a university nearby and I used to think those professors were just lazy, doing nothing of any practical value, and living off the fat of the land. I let more than one of them know that I resented it, that I thought that I was laboring at my business sometimes seven days a week, ten or twelve hours a day so they could do research and write books that didn't have a thing to do with anything real.*
>
> *But while the doctors were saying I was dead, this person I was with, this light, the Christ, showed me a dimension of knowledge, I'll call it. I can't explain it any way to you, but that's all right because every person on earth will see it for himself soon enough, whether they believe it now or not.*
>
> *Now that was a humbling experience for me. You can say I don't scorn professors anymore. Knowledge is important. I read everything I can get my hands on now, I really do. It's not that I regret taking the path I did in life, but I'm glad that I have time now for learning. History, science, literature. I'm interested in it all. My wife fusses at me about my books in our room. Some of it helps me understand my experience better, I would say. All of it does, in one way or another, because, as I say, when you have one of these experiences, you see that everything is connected.*

A New Feeling of Control

All NDEers feel more responsible for the course of their lives. They are also acutely sensitive to the immediate and long-term consequences of their actions. It is the dramatic "life review," with its third-person quality that allows them to examine their life objectively.

NDEers tell me that the life review lets them look at their life as though it were a movie on a screen. Frequently, they can feel the emotions associated with the action they are viewing, not only their own, but also those of the people around them. They can see seemingly unrelated events become connected and witness their "rights" and "wrongs" with crystal clarity. This experience has taught them that at the end of their life, they will have to be the agent and recipient of their every action.

I have yet to meet a person who has been through this experience who doesn't acknowledge that it has made him more careful in choosing his actions. But I don't mean that it has made him neurotically guilty. The sense of responsibility is a positive one that doesn't manifest itself in guilty apprehension.

A woman who had an NDE on her twenty-third birthday, shortly after finishing her graduate education in sociology, told me:

> The most important thing I learned from this experience was that I am responsible for everything I do. Excuses and avoidance were impossible when I was there with him reviewing my life. And not only that, I saw that responsibility is not bad in the least, that I can't make excuses or try to put my failings off on somebody else. It's funny, but my failings have become very dear to me in a way, because they are my failings, and darn it, I am going to learn from them, come hell or high water.
>
> I remember one particular incident in this review when, as a child, I yanked my little sister's Easter basket away from her, because there was a toy in it that I wanted. Yet in the review, I felt her feelings of disappointment and loss and rejection.

What we do to other people when we act unlovingly! But it is wonderful that we are destined not to be allowed to remain unconscious of it. If anybody doesn't believe me about this, okay, I'll meet them in the afterlife when they've had a chance to encounter this and then we can discuss it. . . .

Everything you have done is there (in the review) for you to evaluate, and as unpleasant as some parts of it are for you to see, it feels so good to get it all out. In life, you can play around and make excuses for yourself and even cover up, and you can stay miserable, if you want to, by doing all this covering up. But when I was there in that review there was no covering up. I was the very people that I hurt, and I was the very people I helped to feel good. I wish I could find some way to convey to everyone how good it feels to know that you are responsible and to go through something like this where it is impossible not to face it.

It is the most liberated feeling in the world. It is a real challenge, every day of my life, to know that when I die I am going to have to witness every single action of mine again, only this time actually feeling the effects I've had on others. It sure makes me stop and think. I don't dread it. I relish it.

A Sense of Urgency

"Sense of urgency" is a phrase that comes up again and again when I talk to NDEers. Frequently, they are referring to the shortness and fragility of their own lives. But they are often expressing a sense of urgency about a world in which vast destructive powers are in the hands of mere humans.

Why they have these feelings I don't know. But these factors seem to keep people who have had the experience in a state of profound appreciation of life. After the NDE, people tend to declare that life is precious, that it's the "little things" that count, and that life is to be lived to its fullest.

One woman told me that the life review doesn't show just the big events of one's life, as you might think. She said that it shows the little things, too. For instance, one of the incidents that came across very powerfully in her review was a time when she found a little girl lost in a department store. The girl was crying, and the woman set her up on a counter and talked to her until her mother arrived.

It was those kinds of things—the little things you do while not even thinking—that come up most importantly in the review.

Many people are asked by the being, "What was in your heart while this was going on?" It's as though he's telling the NDEer that the simple acts of kindness that come from the heart are the ones that are most important because they are most sincere.

Better Developed Spiritual Side

An NDE almost always leads to spiritual curiosity. Many NDEers study and accept the spiritual teachings of the great religious thinkers.

However, this doesn't mean that they become pillars of the local church. To the contrary, they tend to abandon religious doctrine purely for the sake of doctrine.

A very succinct and thought-provoking account of this attitude was given to me by a man who had studied at a seminary before his NDE.

My doctor told me I "died" during the surgery. But I told him that I came to life. I saw in that vision what a stuck-up ass I was with all that theology, looking down on everyone who wasn't a member of my denomination or didn't subscribe to the theological beliefs that I did.

A lot of people I know are going to be surprised when they find out that the Lord isn't interested in theology. He seems to find some of it amusing, as a matter of fact, because he wasn't interested at all in anything about my denomination. He wanted to know what was in my heart, not my head.

Reentering the "Real" World

This readjustment to the mundane world has been dubbed "reentry syndrome" by some researchers. Why shouldn't NDEers have difficulty readjusting? Once you've experienced a spiritual paradise, wouldn't returning to the world be a drag for anyone?

Over two thousand years ago, Plato addressed this syndrome in *The Republic.* In that book, he invites us to imagine a subterranean world in which prisoners are held from birth, manacled and facing the back wall of a cavern, so that they can see only shadows from objects that move in front of the blazing fire behind them.

Suppose, he reasons, one of these prisoners was freed from his bonds and drawn upward, out of the cave entirely, into our world and its beauty. If he was then forced down into the world of shadows, Plato says, he would be ridiculed and derided by the prisoners who had never left the cave when he told them of his experiences. On top of such ridicule, he would have trouble conforming to the dogma of a now more restrictive world.

It is these problems that I deal with in my psychiatric practice. I started what I call a "spiritual practice" in 1985 when I realized that many of the people who had unusual spiritual experiences had difficulty integrating them into their lives.

For instance, many people won't listen to the NDEer's experience. They are disturbed by the event and perhaps even think that the person is insane. But from the NDEers' perspective, something very important has happened, changing their lives, and no one will listen to them sympathetically. Hence, they simply need someone who understands the experience to listen to them.

Amazingly, NDEers usually receive little support from their spouses or family when it comes to dealing with their experience. Often the marked personality changes that go with the NDE cause tension in the family. For instance, some people who have repressed their emotions for years in their marriage suddenly become very open after an NDE. This can be very embarrassing to the spouse. For them, it is almost like being married to a different person.

One man told me:

> When I "came back," no one knew quite what to make of me. When I had my heart attack, I had been a very driven and angry type A. If things didn't go right for me, I was impossible to live with. That was at home as well as work. If my wife wasn't dressed on time when we had some place to go, I would blow up and make the rest of the evening miserable for her.
>
> Why she put up with it, I don't know. I guess she grew accustomed to it over the years, though, because after my NDE she could hardly cope with my mellowness. I didn't yell at her anymore. I didn't push her to do things, or anyone else for that matter. I became the easiest person to live with and the change was almost more than she could bear. It took a lot of patience on my part—which is something I had never possessed before—to keep our marriage together. She kept saying, "You are so different since your heart attack." I think she really wanted to say, "You've gone crazy."

To relieve these stresses, I occasionally bring a group of NDEers and their spouses together so they can share with others the effects of the NDE on their family life. They find that other people are having the same problems that they are, and they try to learn how to cope with the new person.

Another thing that happens to NDEers is that they almost long for the blissful state of existence that they discovered in their NDE. When they come back to this realm, they miss the other place. They have to learn to deal with this longing.

In 1983, I conducted a conference on coping with an NDEer that was attended by dozens of medical professionals experienced in dealing with NDEers. In the course of that three-day gathering, we came up with several guidelines in dealing with these spiritual crises. I am including them here so you can see some of the aspects involved in coping with an NDE.

- *Let NDEers talk freely about their experience.* Listen sympathetically and let them talk about their near-death experience as much as they will. Don't use this occasion to try to alleviate your own worries about life after death or to prove any of your own theories about it. The NDEer has had an intense experience, and he or she needs an open ear to hear the episode as it was.

- *Reassure them that they're not alone.* Tell them that experiences like this are very common. Tell them also that we don't totally understand why they happen, but that the many others who have had NDEs have grown from the experience.

- *Tell them what the experience is.* Although millions of people have had NDEs, few of them even know what they are called. Tell them that they have had a near-death experience. By having the clinical name for their episode, the NDEer will have a handle on understanding this bewildering and unexpected event.

• *Bring the family into the picture.* The changes NDEs bring to people frequently are difficult for their families to cope with. A father who may have been a hard-driving type-A before an NDE will suddenly become a mellow type-B after the incident. Such a change can be difficult for a family accustomed to the head of the house being demanding and "tightly wound."

It's important to encourage family dialogue to make sure that everyone's feelings about this change become known so they can be coped with before they cause a rift in the family structure.

• *Meet other NDEers.* I frequently have a new NDEer meet other NDEers. Over the years I have run several group therapy sessions with NDEers. They are brought together by physician referral. Ideally, the group would be about four people who simply talk over the problems caused by their NDE.

These group sessions are among the most amazing I have ever attended. The people in them are plainly talking about a common event, not some illusion, fantasy, or dream. It's almost as though they have taken a voyage to another country together.

I frequently invite the spouses of NDE patients to these group sessions, since being around other NDEers and their spouses is reassuring for them. Researchers have shown divorce often follows an NDE because the person undergoes so many personality changes. By being around others in the same situation, new NDEers and their spouses can see how others have fit these episodes into their family life.

Of course, some people are delighted to have a "mellower" spouse around the house. But others are not. Although they have been saying to the person for years that they wished he would calm down, when he does, they really don't like it. They may interpret this transformation as evidence of a psychosis or diminished vigor.

The International Association for Near-Death Studies (IANDS) sponsors NDE support groups across the country, currently in nearly thirty cities. For information on a group near you, write to "Friends of IANDS," Department of Psychiatry, University of Connecticut Health Center, Farmington, CT 06032.

• *Have NDEers read about the experience.* This type of therapy is called *bibliotherapy,* and it is usually not recommended by psychiatrists or psychologists. The reason for this is that most patients don't find it soothing to read about their psychological problems. After all, patients with schizophrenia wouldn't find it calming to see the symptoms of their disease printed in black and white. NDEs are very different, however, since they are considered spiritual experiences and not a disease.

I have found that later on, after they have had time to integrate the experience themselves, it's important to refer them to good books on the subject. That way they get the opportunity to review the variety of experiences and thoughts on the subject at their leisure.

The aim of this is to help the person fit this experience into his life and make sure that the certain change that comes with a near-death experience is a positive and growing one.

What little research there is on the subject shows the changes to be quite positive. This research shows that whether NDEs are voyages into the otherworld or something less, they have very strong effects on the people who have them. Or, as one sociologist put it: "Things are real when they are real in their consequence."

CHAPTER 3

Children and NDEs: Meeting the Guardian Angel

The near-death experiences of children have special meaning. In dealing with such innocents, researchers have the opportunity to examine individuals who have spent very little time thinking about life, death, and the hereafter. Since children are not steeped in the speculations of the adult world around them, they have no knowledge of anything resembling a near-death experience.

It is because these children are freer of cultural conditioning than adults that their episodes add validity to the core near-death experience.

Even at very early ages—as early as six months, as you'll read later—children report the same symptoms in their NDEs as do adults from all cultures: the sensation of seeing one's own body from a vantage point outside the physical body; panoramic life review; entering a tunnel; meeting others, including living and dead relatives; encountering a being of light; sensing the presence of a deity; and returning to one's body.

From the mouths of babes comes wisdom is an axiom that well applies to children who have NDEs, as it does to so many things in life.

My First NDE Child

My first NDE child came to me as a surprise while I was a resident in a Georgia hospital. I was performing a routine examination on a patient I'll call Sam, a nine-year-old who almost died the previous year from a cardiac arrest due to an adrenal gland disease.

I was chatting with him about his illness when he shyly volunteered: "About a year ago, I died."

I began to coax him about his experience. He told me that after he died, he floated out of his body and looked down as the doctor pushed on his chest to restart his heart. Sam, in his altered state, tried to get the doctor to quit hitting him, but the doctor wouldn't pay any attention.

At that point, Sam had the experience of moving upward very rapidly and seeing the earth fall away below him.

He then passed through a dark tunnel and was met on the other side by a group of "angels." I asked him if these angels had wings and he said no.

"They were glowing," he said, luminescent, and all of them seemed to love him very much.

Everything in this place was filled with light, he said. Yet through it all, he saw beautiful, pastoral scenes. This heavenly place was surrounded by a fence. He was told by the angels that if he went beyond the fence he wouldn't be able to return to life. He was then told by a being of light (Sam called him God) that he had to go back and reenter his body.

"I didn't want to go back but he made me," said Sam.

This conversation was especially exciting to me. When

individuals have an NDE at a very early age, it seems to get incorporated into their personality. It is something they live with all their lives and it changes them. No longer are they afraid of death the way their peers are. Instead, they have the air of someone who has seen our next existence.

These insights make them very sensitive and mature people who approach life in an unusually mature way. They will frequently express a nostalgia for the experience down through the years. And when things get rough for them, they will take comfort in, as one person told me, "having been on the other side."

One man who had an NDE as a child said that in the intervening years, he had been threatened with death twice. One of these experiences was in wartime. Another time he was held down on the floor of a grocery store by a crazed gunman who was robbing the market and was going to kill him as an example to the other captives.

He said that on neither of those occasions was he frightened. The fear he may have felt was replaced by memories of his encounter with the being of light.

"The Light Was Very Bright"

Some researchers have concluded that NDEs are the mind's defense mechanism against the fear of dying. But NDEs in children refute that theory, since children have very different perceptions of dying than do adults.

Children under the age of seven, for instance, tend to think of death as temporary, like a vacation period, perhaps. To them, death is something you return from. From about age seven to ten, death is a magical concept, one that gets replaced in the next few years by the knowledge that death involves organic decomposition. During the seven-to-ten period, children personify death. They think of it as a monster or some kind of goblin that is going to eat them up. They think it lurks in the dark and they can run away from it if it comes.

At any rate, the child's perceptions of death are very different from those of the adult. For instance, many older people fear an obliteration of consciousness, while others fear the pain that they imagine they will have to go through during the dying process. Some fear being alone or being cut off from relatives and friends, while others fear hell fire and damnation. Some people fear the loss of control that death implies, that they won't any longer be in charge of their business, family, or whatever it is they are trying to run. Some have the primitive fear of dismemberment.

Children don't have this cultural conditioning yet. And those who have had NDEs usually don't experience these fears later on. They have little fear of death and often speak fondly of their near-death experiences. Some of the children I have talked to have expressed a desire to "return to the light."

One of those children is a nine-year-old girl I'll call Nina. She underwent an NDE during appendicitis surgery. Her surgeons immediately went to work resuscitating her, an event that she suddenly found herself watching from an out-of-body vantage point.

I heard them say my heart had stopped but I was up at the ceiling watching. I could see everything from up there. I was floating close to the ceiling, so when I saw my body I didn't know it was me. Then I knew because I recognized it. I went out in the hall and I saw my mother crying. I asked her why she was crying but she couldn't hear me. The doctors thought I was dead.

Then a pretty lady came up and helped me because she knew I was scared. We went through a tunnel and went into heaven. There are beautiful flowers there. I was with God and Jesus. They said I had to go back to be with my mother because she was upset. They said I had to finish my life. So I went back and I woke up.

The tunnel I went through was long and very dark. I went through it real fast. There was light at the end. When we saw the light I was very happy. I wanted to go back for a long time. I still want to go back to the light when I die. . . . The light was very bright.

Another child who speaks longingly of his NDE is a boy I'll call Jason. He had an NDE after being hit by a car while riding his bicycle. His episode is an interesting "full-blown" NDE in that it exhibits many of the symptoms of the core experience and is a very intense one.

I spoke to him when he was fourteen, three years after his event. Although his accident was a bad one, tests have shown that there was no brain damage. And, as you can see, his answers are sharp and intelligent.

Jason: This happened when I was eleven. I got a new bike for my birthday. The day after my birthday, I was riding the bike and I didn't see a car coming and it hit me.

I don't remember getting hit but suddenly I was looking down at myself. I saw my body under the bike and my leg was broken and bleeding. I remember looking and seeing my eyes closed. I was above.

I was floating about five feet above my body and there were people all around. A man in the crowd tried to help me. An ambulance came. I wondered why the people were worried because I was fine. I watched them put my body in the ambulance and I was trying to tell them it was fine but none of them could hear me. I could tell what they were saying. "Help him," someone was saying. "I think he's dead, but let's go to work," said someone else.

The ambulance drove off and I tried to follow it. I was

above the ambulance following it. I thought I was dead. I looked around and then I was in a tunnel with a bright light at the end. The tunnel seemed to go up and up. I came out on the other side of the tunnel.

There were a lot of people in the light but I didn't know any of them. I told them about the accident and they said I had to go back. They said it wasn't my time to die yet so I had to go back to my father and mother and sister.

I was in the light for a long time. It seemed like a long time. I felt everyone loved me there. Everyone was happy. I feel that the light was God. The tunnel whirled up toward the light like a whirlpool. I didn't know why I was in the tunnel or where I was going. I wanted to get to that light. When I was in the light I didn't want to go back. I almost forgot about my body.

When I was going up in the tunnel two people were helping me. I saw them as they got out into the light. They were with me the whole way.

Then they told me I had to go back. I went back through the tunnel where I ended up back in the hospital where two doctors were working on me. They said, "Jason, Jason." I saw my body on this table and it looked blue. I knew I was going to go back because the people in the light told me.

The doctors were worried, but I was trying to tell them I was all right. One doctor put paddles on my chest and my body bounced up.

When I woke up I told the doctor I saw him when he put the paddles on my chest. I tried to tell my mother too, but no one wanted to hear it. I told my teacher in class one day and she told you.

Moody: Jason, what do you make of all this? I mean, this happened to you three years ago. Has it changed you in anyway? What do you think it means?

Jason: Well, I have thought a lot about it. To me I died. I saw the place where you go when you die. I am not afraid of dying. What I learned there is that the most important thing is loving while you are alive.

Last year a boy in my class died. He had leukemia. Nobody wanted to talk about it but I said that Don is okay where he is, that death is not that big a thing. I told them about when I died, and that is why my teacher told you.

Moody: Jason, did you notice anything about the people in the tunnel with you?

Jason: The two people with me in the tunnel helped me as soon as I got there. I didn't know where I was exactly but I wanted to get to that light at the end. They told me I would be okay and they would take me into the light. I could feel love from them. I didn't see their faces, just shapes in the tunnel. When we got into the light I could see their faces. This is hard to explain because this is very different from life in the world. I don't have any word for it. It was like they were wearing very white robes. Everything was lighted.

Moody: You said they talked to you. What did they say?

Jason: No. I could tell what they were thinking and they could tell what I was thinking.

Moody: At some point you said you were dead. Could you tell me about that?

Jason: You mean when I was floating over the ambulance? I was looking down from above the ambulance. I knew my body was in the ambulance but there I was above it. One of the men in the ambulance said he thought I was dead and when I spoke to them nobody heard me, so I knew I was dead. As soon as I knew I was dead this tunnel opened up and I saw the light at the end. When I went in there was this "swoosh." It was fun being there.

Children's obviously pleasant memories of their NDEs is a healthy sign. Very often these children form attachments to the people they met on "the other side." When they come back, they talk about the beautiful woman who took care of them when they died.

To me this is one more indication of the NDE's positive

effects, even on a "culturally unconditioned" segment of society. The experience neither causes fear nor affects children like a mental illness; rather, young NDEers usually form a sort of attachment to their episodes. This "longing for the beautiful light," as one patient told me, has made most child NDEers better people as they grow older. Once again, it's their special knowledge that makes them kinder and more patient.

An older patient who had an NDE as a child told me:

> I never got wrapped up in family bickering like my brothers and sisters did. My mother said it was because I "had the bigger picture." I suppose that might have been true.
>
> I just knew though that nothing we were arguing about had any real importance. After meeting the Being of Light, I knew that any arguing that went on was meaningless. So when anything like that started in the family, I would just curl up with a book and let other people work out their problems. Mine had already been worked out for me. I am the same way, even now—more than thirty years after it happened to me.

Other Researchers' Conclusions

There is little medical research that deals with children and NDEs. But what there is certainly deserves to be examined, since researchers have come to their own conclusions about the meaning of NDEs in the very young.

One such researcher is Dr. David Herzog of Massachusetts General Hospital in Boston. In a case report entitled "Near-Death Experiences in the Very Young,"[*] Herzog reports on a six-month-old girl who was admitted to the intensive care

[*]Herzog, "Near-Death Experiences in the Very Young," *Critical Care Medicine*, Vol. 13, No. 12, p. 1074.

unit with a severe illness. She was immediately given proper therapy, including oxygen for stabilization, and in a short period of time she was well again.

However, several months later, she panicked when encouraged by her brothers and sisters to crawl through a tunnel at a local department store. Dr. Herzog, who identifies this fear as "tunnel panic," says that the problem occurred on several subsequent occasions.

"According to her mother," reads the case report, "during these episodes the patient would talk very fast, be unduly frightened and overwhelmed and would seem as if she knew the tunnel quite well. At the age of three and a half, when her mother was explaining the impending death of the grandmother, the child replied, 'Will Grandma have to go through the tunnel at the store to get to see God?' "

Although Herzog acknowledges that the imagery of the tunnel is the same as that experienced by adults, he avoids interpreting the meaning of the episode. Rather, he points out the need for immediate understanding, comfort, and reassurance by the doctors and parents of an NDE.

"Helping the child express his emotions and understand his reactions to past traumatic events will allow him to resolve earlier fears and past trauma."

Another case study comes from Dr. Melvin Morse of The Children's Orthopedic Hospital and Medical Center in Seattle. He reports on a seven-year-old girl who nearly drowned in a local swimming pool.

Morse first saw the girl when she was brought to the emergency room. He gave her the appropriate medication and put her on a respirator for three days. After a week in the hospital, she was released.

She admitted to having an NDE about two weeks later during a follow-up examination. Asked what she remembered of the experience, she told the doctor that she only remembered "talking to the Heavenly Father." She then became too embarrassed to discuss it further.

A week later, Morse interviewed her. She was embarrassed when he first mentioned the NDE, but decided to discuss the episode with him because "it feels good to talk about it." She wouldn't allow the interview to be tape-recorded and would only talk about the incident after first drawing pictures of what had happened. To quote from Morse's paper:

> The patient said that the first memory she had of her near-drowning was "being in the water." She stated, "I was dead. Then I was in the tunnel. It was dark and I was scared. I couldn't walk." A woman named Elizabeth appeared, and the tunnel became bright. The woman was tall, with bright yellow hair. Together they walked to heaven. She stated that "heaven was fun. It was bright and there were lots of flowers." She said that there was a border around heaven that she could not see past. She said that she met many people including her dead grandparents, her dead maternal aunt, and Heather and Melissa, two adults waiting to be reborn. She then met the "Heavenly Father and Jesus," who asked her if she wanted to return to earth. She replied "no." Elizabeth then asked her if she wanted to see her mother. She said yes and woke up in the hospital. Finally, she claimed to remember seeing me in the emergency room, but could not supply any other details of the three-day period during which she was comatose.*

Morse delves into the patient's religious background. Being a Mormon, the girl was taught that earth is but a stopping place on the way to heaven. She was told that she would eventually be reunited with her dead relatives, including her aunt who had died two years before her near drowning.

*Morse, "A Near-Death Experience in a Seven-Year-Old Child," *The American Journal of the Disabled Child*, Vol. 137, pp. 959–961.

Her mother had described death as "saying good-bye to people on the sailboat. We can only go to the edge and wave to them." The soul was described to her as being like a glove that comes off your hand at death and joins you again in heaven.

Morse admits that events during his patient's NDE— meeting Jesus, seeing dead relatives—neatly meshes with her religious training. But despite such religious training, he points out that her experience is the same as that of many nonreligious people who have had NDEs. Just as they experienced passing through a tunnel, seeing beings of light, talking to a deity, and viewing heaven, so did she.

He concludes—as have other researchers—that religious background doesn't alter the core experience, only the interpretation of the experience.

More from Morse

Since reporting on this case in 1983, Dr. Morse continued studying NDEs in children.

In 1985, he published a study entitled "Near-Death Experiences in a Pediatric Population," in which he interviewed seven children who were three to sixteen years old when they were "critically ill," (that is, suffering from conditions with high mortality rates). In most of these, the children had cardiac arrests caused by trauma or near drowning. Other patients in the same age group but who had serious (not necessarily life-threatening) conditions were interviewed, too. They experienced no NDE episodes.

The children were interviewed at least two months after leaving the hospital. They were accompanied by their parents, who were asked for their perception of the child's medical history. Then both the parent(s) and child were asked open-ended questions about the child's memories of his or her hospitalization. There were questions like: "Did you have dreams?" "What do you remember about the time you were unconscious or asleep?" The children were also encouraged to draw pictures of their experiences.

When the interview was almost completed, the children were asked a series of yes and no questions about NDE symptoms like: "Did you see a tunnel?" "Did you see a being of light?"

Four of the seven critically ill patients reported NDEs. Two of those four said the NDE had a peaceful effect, two had out-of-body experiences, one saw a bright tunnel and another a dark staircase; two were asked by the being of light if they wanted to stay in this heavenly place and made decisions to return.

Some of the interviews were quite startling. One of the patients who "died" of a cardiac arrest on the operating table told his parents, "I have a wonderful secret to tell you. I have been halfway to heaven." He said he "was on a dark staircase" and "climbed upwards." About halfway up, he decided to turn back because he had a younger brother who had died and he didn't think it was his time to join him yet because his parents would be lonely.

From this study, Morse concluded that children have much the same NDEs as do adults. He also hoped that the study would "alert" other doctors that these experiences occur to a "significant number of critically ill children." But the study also encouraged him to look into another intriguing question: Does a person have to be near death to have an NDE, or can one have the experience with an illness that isn't life threatening?

Dr. Morse attempted to answer this question with his next study. In that work, researchers culled through 202 medical records to find eleven patients who had survived "critical illnesses," which were defined as conditions with a mortality rate greater than 10 percent. Also studied were twenty-nine patients of the same age who had survived "serious illnesses," those with very small mortality rates.

Although none of the seriously ill had NDEs, seven of the eleven critically ill had memories that included being out of their body (six patients), entering darkness (five), peaceful or positive effects (three), seeing people or beings dressed in white (three), visions of classmates or teachers (two), visions of dead relatives (one), reaching a border (one), being in a tunnel (four), and deciding to return to their body (three).

The interviews were conducted in a similar fashion to the ones Dr. Morse did in the study on children and NDEs. But the answers were far more interesting. An eleven-year-old boy, for instance, had a cardiac arrest in the lobby of a hospital. Suddenly, according to the study:

He remembers being in the hospital lobby and then feeling a sinking feeling "like when you go over a bump in a car and your stomach drops out from under you." He heard a "whooshing" noise in his ears and people talking. He then was floating on the ceiling of the room looking down at his body below him. The room was dim, and his body was illuminated by a soft light. He heard a nurse say, "I wish we didn't have to do this," and observed ongoing cardiopulmonary resuscitation. He saw a nurse "put some grease on my body," and then she "handed paddles to the doctor." The paddles were placed on his body and when "the doctor pressed the button, I was suddenly back in my body, looking up at the doctor."

He perceived significant pain as the shock went through his body and stated that he had recurrent nightmares of the pain of this technique, known as cardioversion.

Nurses present at the event state that he opened his eyes after cardioversion and said, "That was really weird. I was

floating above my body and was sucked back into myself."
He had no memory of making that statement.

Another of the interview subjects remembered a being about eight feet tall who took him through a tunnel. "It wasn't Christ," he assured Morse. "It may have been an angel though, taking me to Christ."

Morse's conclusion was that the core NDE is experienced only by people surviving critical illness or those undergoing life-threatening stress.

I Saw Myself as an Adult

Over the last couple of years, I've started asking children how old they are *during the NDE.* In other words, is their spirit body one of a child or an adult? A surprising number of them say that they are adults during the episode, although they can't say how they know this.

If you believe in the NDE as the spirit leaving its earthly body, then it could mean that the spirit itself is an ageless entity that finds itself housed in an ever-changing body. When it finally wears a body out, it goes to another world.

Another possible explanation is that these children are made to feel so comfortable by the beings of light, that they feel as though they are among peers. This could lead to them thinking they are the same age as those around them.

One woman told me about one such NDE she had as a child.

It was around noon one day when I was seven years old, and I was on my way home from school to eat lunch. There was a patch of ice in the middle of the road and I ran to slide on it as kids will do. Well, when I hit it, my feet ran out from under me and I hit my head. I got up and walked the three blocks home, but I wasn't coherent at all.

My mother asked me what was wrong and I told her that I had slipped and hit my head. She gave me an aspirin, but when I went to take it, I couldn't find my mouth.

Right away, she made me lie down and she called the doctor. It was then that I passed out. I was out for twelve hours and they didn't know whether I was going to live or die in that period of time.

Of course, I don't remember any of that. All I remember was waking up in a garden filled with large flowers. If I had to describe them, I would say they looked like big, tall dahlias. It was warm and light in this garden and it was beautiful.

I looked around the garden and saw this being. The garden was extraordinarily beautiful, but everything paled in his presence. I felt completely loved and completely nourished by his presence. It was the most delightful feeling I've ever known. And although it was several years ago, I can still feel that feeling.

The being said to me—without words—"So, you're going back." And I answered in the same way, "Yes." He asked me why I wanted to return to my body and I said, "Because my mother needs me."

At that moment, I remember going down a tunnel and the light kept getting smaller and smaller. And when I couldn't see light anymore, I woke up.

I got up and looked around and I said, "Hello, mother."

In looking back at the experience, I realize that I was fully mature when I was in his presence. As I said, I was only seven but I know I was an adult.

As NDE research advances, we will eventually be able to find out how widespread this phenomenon is.

Conclusion

For many, the near-death experiences of children give better evidence for a life after death than those that occur in older people. It isn't hard to understand why. Older people have had more time to be influenced and shaped by their life's experiences and a myriad of religious beliefs.

Children have, on the other hand, come to the experience with a certain freshness. They haven't had time to be deeply influenced by the cultural material they are rapidly becoming surrounded by.

But on the clinical level, the most important aspect of child NDEs is the glimpse of the "life beyond" that they receive and how it affects them for the rest of their lives. They are happier and more hopeful than those around them. They present even stronger evidence that NDEs are positive transformations in a person's life.

CHAPTER 4

Why Near-Death Experiences Intrigue Us

Up to now, we have been dealing with the effects of the near-death experience on the people who have them. But how does it affect people around the NDEer? And why is the public so fascinated by the near-death experience?

Frankly, when I wrote *Life After Life* more than ten years ago, I wouldn't have thought that public interest in NDEs would continue so long and strong. I thought it would be one of those areas of science that disappeared into the research labs and medical classrooms, only to emerge when a patient experienced an NDE and needed explanation and counseling.

But, even though the explanations for the phenomenon of the near-death experience aren't necessarily clearer, public interest has grown unabated. In my travels to different conferences and public gatherings, people still want answers to many of the basic questions about near-death experiences:

- Are NDEers really dead?

- How do NDEers regard their bodies?

- Does the NDE act as religious confirmation?

- Do NDEs appear in literature?

- How can "combat NDEs" be explained?

- Can NDEs provide hope for the grief stricken?

- How do NDEs affect the suicidal?

- Would science be altered by proving NDE?

- Do NDEs intrigue simply because they are new and faddish?

In this chapter, I plan to answer these questions to the best of my ability. But first I want to show why near death can be more disturbing to the living than death itself.

Several years ago, a psychiatrist told me of an incident that occurred on a plane as he was returning home to the United States after a visit to India.

As dinner was being served, a passenger became very ill. There were several physicians aboard who came forward to help. But despite their best attempts at resuscitation, the man appeared to have died.

His body was left in the aisle and covered with blankets. Soon, the excited curiosity of the other passengers calmed and, incredibly enough, they continued to eat their dinners.

After a few minutes, several passengers seated near the body noticed twitching and stirring underneath the blankets. They called again for the physicians, who rushed forward and this time were able to resuscitate the man, who survived.

What the psychiatrist noticed at that point was that no one continued eating. When he asked questions of those around him, he found that the people on the plane were more disturbed by a return from the dead than the apparently more accepted state of death itself.

The message is clear: we human beings have spent our lives laying down boundaries. We are far more prepared to deal with death than a seeming return from it. We assign some phenomena to one side of our mental boundaries and some to the other. As children we learn the differences between girls and boys, for instance. And later in life we are often quite confused by people who cross the line that divides the sexes, be they transsexuals or transvestites.

We believe that "one body, one self" is a natural law. So when we discover multiple personalities such as the famous ones named Eve and Sybil, our mental boundaries are broken by the thought that more than one self could inhabit the same body.

We learn that a human is one thing and an animal something else. So when children are found who have been raised by wolves or apes, our boundaries are challenged and we are disturbed deeply. The same is true of our fascination with such things as Siamese twins and the Elephant Man. They challenge our boundaries about how we think the world should be and make us question those values that we have always held true.

The relationship of all this to the question of why we are so intrigued by NDEs should be clear.

The line between life and death is the most worrisome of all. We learn that death is something to be avoided. We try to keep thoughts of death out of our consciousness and usually learn gradually the meaning of death.

It is this dividing line between life and death that is challenged by the NDE. Many times over the past twenty years, I have watched the fascination on the faces in an audience as someone recounted his or her near-death experience. It seems as though many people never become accustomed to the idea that a person standing before them has not only "returned from the dead," but has witnessed something spiritual that many people identify as an afterlife.

Are NDEers Really Dead?

Once, after a lecture I gave on my work, an elderly woman came to me from the audience. She had lost her husband about a year before, she said. He had died of a heart attack after the doctors tried for some time to revive him. After hearing about NDEers who had experienced heart attacks and were resuscitated, she had but two thoughts on her mind: Had the doctors given up too soon on her husband? And how close to death are NDEers?

I stepped gingerly around her first question. Since I wasn't there, I declared, it would be impossible to tell whether or not all that could have been done was done.

The second question—"Are NDEers ever really dead?"— is a difficult one to answer. Many times resuscitation attempts have been stopped because the doctors could detect no vital signs. Other times, EEG monitors attached to the brain registered straight lines, which means there is no recordable sign of brain wave activity. Yet sometimes these people return, and no one in medicine can really say why.

By the classical definition, death is the state from which you don't return. It is defined as irreversible. Hence, since all of the NDEers returned, they were never really dead. What happened was that various criteria of death were fulfilled. For instance, their heart stopped beating for a length of time, or they weren't breathing. There are even certain instances in which brain waves stop and then spontaneously begin again. Some people who experience hypothermia (a dramatic lowering of body temperature) show no signs of brain wave activity until they begin to warm up again.

Although they are very near death, by definition they aren't there yet. Many of these situations bring into question the five-minute rule, which states that if the heart stops for more than five minutes, there is no reason to continue resuscitation because the brain would be hopelessly starved of oxygen. With modern resuscitation techniques, this rule of thumb may have to be reconsidered.

One man I know was severely injured in an automobile accident and taken to the emergency room of a hospital where he was declared dead on arrival.

His body was placed on a tressel and rolled behind some curtains in the emergency room, where it was left while the doctors went about the business of taking care of the other people injured in the accident. Several hours later, attendants started to wheel the body off to another part of the hospital when the man twitched!

Despite the absence of vital signs such as heartbeat and functioning pupils, this man was alive and is so today.

Another man I know carries around his own obituary. He was brought to the hospital, pronounced dead, and sent to the morgue with a sheet over him. Remarkably, he spontaneously revived a few hours later.

The lesson in all of this is that there is a lot we don't know about the physiology of dying. So technically speaking, NDEers are never really dead, but they are much closer than most of us have ever been.

How Do NDEers Regard Their Bodies?

A near-death experience makes many people think of their bodies in different terms. Most of the NDEers I have talked to regard their bodies as a house for their spirit. As a result, they become less frightened of the world around them and of "outside" opinions about their appearance.

For instance, an NDEer who has become one of my best friends led quite a normal life until she "died" of cardiac arrest during gall bladder surgery. Her physician had vigorously attempted to get her heart started for more than twenty minutes before giving up and ordering the attendants in the room to fill out the death certificate. A flicker of life encouraged him to renew the resuscitation attempt and finally her heart started beating again.

During that time, she experienced a separation from her body and observed the doctor and nurses as they tried to save her life. She rose through a tunnel into a beautiful realm of light and love in which she saw all the events of her life replayed in great detail. She saw relatives and friends who had died years before, and was even given a choice to return or stay. As difficult as the decision was, she chose to return to her present life because of her daughter and husband.

Since that event ten years ago, her physical health has continued to fail. She has diabetes and chronic spine problems that have required several operations for fusion and other repairs.

Still, for as long as I have known her, I have never once heard her complain of pain or suffering. Although she must at times have considerable discomfort, her attitude is one of luminous serenity.

I found out recently that she further crossed the boundaries set down by her ailing body by visiting an amusement park and riding every ride, even the full-loop roller coaster. To me, that was symbolic of her belief in life after death.

Many people who have an out-of-body experience during their NDE don't even recognize the body they left as being their own. Many NDEers have told me that before the experience, they were accustomed to knowing themselves by looking in mirrors and at photographs. But the NDE made them look at their own body in a different way.

One of the most memorable examples of this came from a psychiatrist who had an NDE. He said, "In life, you may think you know what you look like. But when you get out of your body and see your own physical body, it's very difficult to see which one of all the bodies in the world are yours."

In his case, he was wandering around an Army hospital looking at rows of bodies in beds, and he couldn't tell which one was his. He had been out of his body and out of the hospital trying to get home. But when he realized that no one could see or hear him, he came back and began trying to find himself.

He literally had trouble doing that until he discovered a body with his fraternity ring on it and realized it must be his.

Another man I know fell from a billboard onto some high-voltage wires. He lost his legs and part of one arm from the burns. He had an out-of-body experience in the operating room. While looking down at his own body, the first thought that came to his mind was, "Look at that poor man." He didn't even recognize the body on the table as being his own. When he finally realized that badly damaged body was his, he noticed something else peculiar: his spiritual body was not handicapped in anyway.

Many handicapped people who have NDEs find that their handicaps are gone. In the spiritual realm, they are whole and highly mobile beings. It has been my experience that the NDE allows the handicapped to be more accepting of their problems.

Although NDEs make many people think of their bodies as the house for their spirit, I don't mean to imply that they become risk takers as a result of the experience. They don't develop the devil-may-care attitude that many sky divers or rock climbers have. If anything, NDEers become more careful of their bodies.

The NDE As Religious Confirmation

Although some researchers theorize that NDEs are caused by intense belief in God and the hereafter, the fact is that these experiences happen to nonbelievers just as frequently as to believers.

Over the years I have discovered NDEers with all sorts of religious backgrounds. Some people tell me that before the experience they didn't believe in God. Others say that they were very religious.

The interesting thing is that after the NDE, the effect seems to be the same: people who weren't overtly religious before the experience say afterward that they do believe in God and have an appreciation for the spiritual, as do the people who believed in God all along.

Both groups emerge with an appreciation of religion that is different from the narrowly defined one established by most churches. They come to realize through this experience that religion is not a matter of one "right" group versus several "wrong" groups. People who undergo an NDE come out of it saying that religion concerns your ability to love—not doctrines and denominations. In short, they think that God is a much more magnanimous being than they previously thought, and that denominations don't count.

A good example of this is an elderly woman in New Hampshire who had an NDE after a cardiac arrest. She had been a very religious and doctrine-abiding Lutheran since she was a child. But after the NDE, she loosened up and became a more joyous person. When members of her family asked her to account for the change in her personality, she said simply that she understood God after her episode and realized that he didn't care about church doctrine at all.

There are many religions around the world that readily accept NDEs as the doorway to the spiritual world. The most prominent of the Western religions to do this is the Church of the Latter Day Saints, more commonly known as the Mormon Church.

The Mormon doctrine supports the NDE as a peek into the spirit world. They believe that the spirit world is a dimension that can't be perceived by the living, but one that is inhabited by those who have left their physical body.

The Mormon *Journal of Discourses*, a commentary on Mormon beliefs written by church elders, says that the spirit body retains the five senses of the physical body (sight, hearing, feeling, taste, and smell) while having "enhanced capacities" and the ability to consider many different ideas at the same time. It can also move with lightning speed, see in many different directions at the same time, and communicate in many ways other than speech. And it is free of disability and illness.

Mormon doctrine says that the spirit enters the body at birth and leaves upon death. It defines death as "merely a change from one status or sphere of existence to another."

We shall turn around and look upon it (the valley of death) and think when we have crossed it, why this is the greatest advantage of my whole existence, for I have passed from a state of sorrow, grief, mourning, woe, misery, pain, anguish and disappointment into a state of existence where I can enjoy life to the fullest extent as far as that can be done without a body.

Many of the traits of the NDE are described by Mormon leaders. One says, "the brightness and glory of the next apartment is inexpressible," which is basically the same as being engulfed by the soothing light. Another says that "there as here, all things will be natural, and you will understand them as you now understand natural things," which is in keeping with many NDEers who experience a kind of universal understanding.

The experience of seeing relatives and friends after death is supported in the *Journal of Discourses*.

We have more friends behind the veil than on this side, and they will hail us more joyfully than you were ever welcomed by your parents and friends in this world, and you will rejoice more when you meet them than you ever rejoiced to see a friend in this life.

Some Mormon leaders say that "some spirits who have experienced death are called back to inhabit their physical bodies again. These persons pass through the natural or temporal death twice."

Perhaps one of the most famous of these Mormon NDEs happened to Jedediah Grant and was recorded by church leader Heber Kimball for the *Journal of Discourses*:

He said to me, Brother Heber, I have been into the spirit world two nights in succession, and of all the dreads that ever came across me, the worst was to have to return to my body, though I had to do it.

Grant's dread came as a result of meeting his deceased wife nd daughter, as well as many friends, while in the spirit world.

He saw his wife, she was the first person that came to him. He saw many that he knew, but did not have conversation with any but his wife Caroline. She came to him and he said that she looked beautiful and had their little child, that died on the plains, in her arms, and said "Mr. Grant, here is little Margaret; you know that the wolves ate her up; but it did not hurt her, here she is all right."

There is also mention of the afterlife in the Bible, where Paul describes the type of body we will have in the other world.

But some man will say, "How are the dead raised up? And with what body do they come?" Thou fool . . . that which thou sowest, thou sowest not that body that shall be, but bare grain. . . . But God giveth . . . seed his own body. . . . There are also celestial bodies, and bodies terrestrial: but the glory of the celestial is one and the glory of the terrestrial is another. . . . So also is the resurrection of the dead. It is sown in corruption, it is raised in incorruption: It is sown in dishonor; it is raised in glory: It is sown in weakness; it is raised in power: It is sown a natural body; it is raised a spiritual body. There is a natural body, and there is a spiritual body. . . . Behold, I show you a mystery: We shall not all sleep, but we shall all be changed. In a moment, in the twinkling of an eye, at the last trumpet: for the trumpet shall sound and the dead shall be raised incorruptible.

1 Corinthians 15:35–52

The NDE in Literature

It should be noted that there is a whole literary and film genre that deals in return from the dead. Unfortunately, most of these examples could be considered of the horror variety, in which the dead return to the land of the living with malice in mind.

Although the NDE does usually involve some sort of return from the dead, the results are quite different from those of a vampire or Frankenstein. Rather than being very disruptive events, NDEs are usually benign. Instead of being dark and frightening, NDEs offer hope and peace.

There are several instances of NDEs in great literature. In Charles Dickens's A *Christmas Carol*, for instance, Ebenezer Scrooge is transformed from a miserly and cynical widower to "as good a friend, as good a master, and as good a man, as the good old city knew," by having a sort of near-death experience.

In that classic story, Scrooge encounters three ghosts—Christmas Past, Present, and Future—who take him on a life review that ends at his own grave site.

The review, in which he is accompanied by these beings of light, transforms Scrooge. He deeply regrets not having shown more love for others. At the end of the experience, he is a changed man, ready to show compassion for others in order to make up for lost time.

There are also references to NDEs in Victor Hugo's wonderful novel, *Les Misérables*. The main character, Jean Valjean, is pursued throughout his life by a policeman for escaping from prison where he was placed for stealing a loaf of bread to feed his sister's hungry child.

Throughout the book he performs major acts of kindness. One of those is taking care of a starving pregnant woman named Fantine, who eventually dies. As Hugo wrote it:

> *Jean Valjean took Fantine's head in his hands and arranged it on the pillow, as mother would have done for her child. . . . This done, he closed her eyes.*
> *The face of Fantine, at this instant, seemed strangely illuminated. Death is the entrance into the great light.*

Of the death of Valjean, Hugo wrote:

From moment to moment, Jean Valjean grew weaker. . . .
The light of the unknown was already visible in his eye.

And then Valjean's last words:

Love each other dearly always. There is scarcely anything
else in the world but that; to love one another. . . . I see a
light . . . I die happy.

Drawing on her own near-fatal bout with influenza, Katherine Anne Porter wrote "Pale Horse, Pale Rider," a despairing story that takes place near the end of World War I.

In Chapter 1, I included comments from an interview she did on the subject of her brush with the afterlife. Here is a portion of "Pale Horse, Pale Rider," in which her character Miranda sees long-dead relatives:

Moving towards her leisurely as clouds through the shim-
mering air came a great company of human beings, and
Miranda saw in an amazement of joy that they were all the
living she had known. Their faces were transfigured, each
in its own beauty, beyond what she remembered of them,
their eyes were clear and untroubled as good weather, and
they cast no shadows. They were pure identities and she
knew them every one without calling their names or remem-
bering what relation she bore to them. They surrounded her
smoothly on silent feet, then turned their entranced faces
again towards the sea, and she moved among them easily
as a wave among waves.

There are many other examples of near-death experiences in literature, from the letters of Ernest Hemingway to the stories of Thornton Wilder. The point is that NDEs themselves have a place in literature, and shouldn't be lumped together with that exciting but unrelated category of horror literature.

Explaining Combat NDEs

It sometimes happens that people have exalted states of being without even having injuries. Rather, they find themselves in the midst of an intensely dangerous situation—combat being the best example—and suddenly find their perceptions extremely altered.

This experience has been confused with NDEs by some people. They then ask the logical question: How can a near-death experience happen to someone who isn't sick or traumatized?

My answer is that the person didn't *have* an NDE. Quite simply, these intense experiences don't involve the traits of an NDE. Things like going down a tunnel and passing into a beautiful realm of light haven't been reported in these so-called combat NDEs. Mostly these involve a brief flashback of events the person has experienced in his life, or of everything suddenly appearing to slow down. Some of these experiences, as you'll see from the example, involve "going somewhere else," possibly to avoid the unpleasant situation they are in. They don't involve the ecstatic state of the NDE, but they certainly are on a continuum with them.

Here's one example of a combat experience related to me by a World War II veteran:

> *This happened to me in Sicily during the invasion of Italy. My platoon was passing through a field when we were pinned down from in front by a German machine gun*

nest. Since I was platoon sergeant, I considered it my job to get rid of the nest so we could continue to advance.

I went far around, using a grove of fruit trees for cover. In about thirty minutes, I had looped around the field and ahead so that I came in behind them. I was ecstatic. There were three of them in this hole that was dug just on the other side of a bridge. They were so involved in keeping the platoon pinned down that none of them was looking behind.

I probably could have gone within six feet of them and not been seen. I thought about doing that, but instead I threw a hand grenade when I got to the top of the bridge.

I remember pulling the pin and preparing to throw it from about twenty yards away. I cocked my arm and just before throwing it right into their hole I yelled, "Here you go, suckers." Then I hit the dirt and waited . . .

. . . And waited, and waited. The grenade didn't go off. It was a dud, as worthless as a rock.

Before I could do anything, they had turned the machine gun on me and started firing. I curled up in a ball and waited for something to hit me, but nothing did. Maybe it was the rise in the bridge that gave me cover, or maybe just good fortune, but nothing that was fired hit me.

But a funny thing happened. As I lay there, I suddenly left my body, and Sicily, for that matter. I "traveled" to a munitions plant in New Jersey, where I floated over an assembly line of women who were putting hand grenades together. I tried to talk to them and tell them to pay attention to their work, but they wouldn't listen. Instead they kept chattering as they did their work.

I felt like I was there for fifteen or twenty minutes. Then I was suddenly back in Italy, laying at the top of this bridge, still alive. By now the Germans thought I was dead and had turned their gun back around. I got up and pulled the pin on another hand grenade and pitched it into their hole. This time it exploded.

The platoon had seen everything and thought I was dead,

so they were surprised to see me walking around. I was very calm about the whole experience, so calm that the company commander sent me to a psychiatrist. I told him what happened and he gave me a clean bill of health and sent me back into battle.

He told me that he had heard of this happening to other men before, and that I should keep the experience to myself so I wouldn't get sent to him again. That's exactly what I did.

As you can see, this experience differs greatly from NDEs and shouldn't be confused with them. It should, however, be studied further, since such experiences happen quite frequently to soldiers in combat and other people in similarly stressful situations.

Hope for the Grief Stricken

The deepest grief of all is the death of a loved one. For many, that grief is greatly relieved by accounts of near-death experiences.

Very soon after *Life After Life* was published, I got a letter from a family whose daughter had been murdered. She was a young, bright professor who had been killed by a burglar whom she had surprised in her home. She was an only child and her parents had been living a hellish existence since her death.

They said that when they read about near-death experiences, they felt much better about their painful loss.

All of us who research NDEs have stories about people who have been reconciled to the death of a loved one by hearing about near-death experiences. I think the NDE makes many grieving people realize that death is a passage into another place, that even though the events leading up to death can be agonizing, once a person gets out of his body there is no pain and, in fact, a great sense of relief. And, based on many NDEs, there will be a reunion with loved ones in the spiritual realm. That alone soothes many people.

The Effects of NDEs on the Suicidal

The best way to address this issue is to look at the effect of NDEs on people who have them as a result of suicide attempts.

Dr. Bruce Greyson has made an extensive study of these people and found that not only having an NDE, but also having knowledge of the existence of NDEs practically erases the desire for suicide.

Dr. Greyson is a doctor of emergency psychiatry at the University of Connecticut and deals with attempted suicides on a daily basis. He finds that if you compare a group of people who have had NDEs as a result of attempting suicide with a group who didn't have NDEs while attempting suicide, you will find that almost none of the NDEers attempt to kill themselves again. On the other hand, a high percentage of the people who didn't have an NDE will try again to commit suicide. So having an NDE tends to resolve suicidal inclinations.

A researcher in New York gave the case studies of NDEers to patients who had attempted suicide. He found that this made the idea of suicide as a solution go away. This experiment has been repeated several times with the same result: exposure to the near-death experience actually kept people from committing suicide.

These results don't surprise me. Loss of hope is often the reason people try to commit suicide. They feel burdened by life and void of spiritual beliefs. NDEs fill that void. Where before these people felt that life led nowhere, they now feel a rich and fulfilling afterlife awaits them. That knowledge has a way of relieving the pain in their lives. It makes them feel that life is worth living.

A friend of mine witnessed this response in a neighbor of his who was essentially committing suicide by self-neglect. In the middle of the day, my friend's telephone went dead. Since most of the neighbors were away at work, he went down the street to ask a reclusive old lady if he could use her telephone to report the problem to the phone company.

He knocked on her kitchen door and heard her shuffle slowly and painfully from another part of the house to reach him. She let him in and, exhausted from the effort, sat down at the kitchen table and began breathing oxygen from a big, green tank.

When he was finished with the call, he talked to her and found that there was nothing medically wrong with her. She was simply old and depressed, she said, and all this sitting around had made her so weak that her doctor gave her a bottle of oxygen to make what little movement she did easier.

My friend refused to accept that explanation. He thought she was simply dying from lack of exercise and decided to give her something that would alter her mood. He went home and brought back a copy of *Life After Life* for her to read.

A few days later, he saw her walking slowly up the street with the book in her hand. She thanked him profusely and said this was the first time she had been out of the house in over a year because it was the first time she felt like it. She no longer felt so bad about old age and its inevitable result, she said. The hope of life after life made her more willing to accept the here and now.

My friend now reports that this woman has become an active gardener and no longer requires the almost constant companionship of those big, green oxygen bottles.

Would Science Be Altered by Proving NDEs?

The world is governed, say the scientists, by a set of natural laws. For example, the notion that gravity holds our feet on the planet is a simplification of the laws of gravity. Another such law states that all life-forms on earth are carbon based. The world of science is based on these and many other assumptions, and much progress has been made because we know and live by these laws.

If we were to open up a new dimension by proving life after death, it would revolutionize science by introducing other dimensions to study scientifically than the ones we know.

For instance, if it were proved that a person could leave his body and travel through walls just by thinking, it would change the way science thinks about communication and travel, not to mention the properties of life.

It would prove a whole other universe, one that is certainly more developed than the one we now live in. The implications of such a find almost defy description. Can you imagine penetrating another dimension and talking to members of civilizations long dead? Or, for that matter, could you imagine the effect that proof of the spirit world would have upon the science of warfare? I think it would make it virtually obsolete.

If we knew that there was a spirit world in which love and knowledge were the only attributes of importance and the things that wars are fought for—money, land, political power—were important only here on earth, it would certainly change our attitudes and beliefs about the people we consider enemies.

It would make us look at these people in a new light. After all, existence of a spirit world would mean that we would be destined to spend eternity with these people. It would also mean that in our life after life, we would be able to know exactly how they felt about life on earth and about us. Just knowing that such a realm exists would surely make us more tolerant of each other.

There is one problem with NDEs: As it now stands, they are just anecedotal evidence. It has not been possible to scientifically duplicate them or study them on a *closer level* than what we could call "word of mouth." Until the NDE phenomenon can be duplicated, science can't accept these stories as proof of anything but the existence of something that happens to people who almost die.

Although these anecdotes have been extremely convincing to me and a host of other physicians, until they can be successfully replicated, NDEs can always be called into question.

Do NDEs Intrigue Because They Are "Hip"?

Some people say that NDEs are of interest to the public because they are something new. My book *Life After Life* is cited by some as being the first recorded history of the near-death experience. Because of the perceived newness of the subject, some people think interest will wane, and NDEs will go the way of the Hula Hoop or the Edsel.

Actually, neither one of these is true. There are cases of NDEs far back in history, all the way back to references in Plato's *Republic*, written in early Greece.

There are many more NDE accounts now than there were two decades ago, thanks to the development of cardiopulmonary resuscitation. This life-saving technique is allowing us to bring many more people back from the brink of death than would have ever survived before.

The great majority of the people with whom I have talked would have died thirty or forty years ago rather than be revived. So instead of NDEs being merely quaint curiosities in obscure medical journals, like they were several years ago, we can now find hundreds and thousands of people who have been through this experience.

Another difference is that people are much more willing to talk about their experiences openly. Today people are less afraid of being branded kooks by a doctor. And, of course, they certainly don't have to worry about being locked up in a mental hospital anymore, as they might have been thirty years ago.

Now people talk about peculiar experiences. And when they do, they get social support from other NDEers.

However, since we are looking for historic parallels, the first "Life After Life" accounts that I am aware of are contained in Gregory the Great's *Dialogues*, a set of spiritual writings by this sixth-century pope.

In the final book of *Dialogues*, there are forty-two anecdotes that provide "proof" of the soul's immortality. These are a variety of deathbed visions, ghost stories, and near-death accounts. Most of these have been embellished by Gregory to provide the opportunity for heavy moralizing.

In the following account, a soldier "dies" and returns with a powerful tale of the afterlife and the fate of a Constantinople businessman named Stephen.

A certain soldier in this city of ours happened to be struck down (by a plague). He was drawn out of his body and lay lifeless, but he soon returned and described what befell him. At that time there were many people experiencing these things. He said that there was a bridge, under which ran a black, gloomy river which breathed forth an intolerable foul-smelling vapor. But across the bridge there were delightful meadows carpeted with green grass and sweet-smelling flowers. The meadows seemed to be meeting places for people clothed in white. Such a pleasant odor filled the air that the sweet smell by itself was enough to satisfy [all the needs of] the inhabitants who were strolling there. In that place each one had his own separate dwelling, filled with magnificent light. A house of amazing capacity was being constructed there, apparently out of golden bricks, but he could not find out for whom it might be. On the bank of the river there were dwellings, some of which were contaminated by the foul vapor that rose up from the river, but others were not touched at all.

On the bridge there was a test. If any unjust person wished to cross, he slipped and fell into the dark and stinking water. But the just, who were not blocked by guilt, freely and easily made their way across to the region of delight. He revealed that he saw Peter, an elder of the ecclesiastical family, who died four years ago; he lay in the horrible slime underneath the bridge, weighed down by an enormous iron chain. When he asked why this should be, [he] was given an answer that called to our minds exactly what we know of this man's deeds. He was told, "He suffers these things because whenever he was ordered to punish someone he used to inflict blows more out of a love of cruelty than out of obedience." No one who knew him is unaware that he behaved this way.

He also saw a certain pilgrim priest approach the bridge and cross it with as much self-command in his walk as there was sincerity in his life. On the same bridge, he claimed to have recognized that Stephen of whom we spoke before. In his attempt to cross the bridge, Stephen's foot slipped, and the lower half of his body was now dangling off the bridge. Some hideous men came up from the river and grabbed him by the hips to pull him down. At the same time, some very splendid men dressed in white began to pull him up by the arms. While the struggle went on, with good spirits pulling him up and evil spirits dragging him down, the one who was watching all this was sent back to his body. So he never learned the outcome of the struggle.

What happened to Stephen can, however, be explained in terms of his life. For in him the evils of the flesh contended with the good work of almsgiving. Since he was dragged down by the hips and pulled up by the arms, it is plain to see that he loved almsgiving and yet did not refrain completely from the carnal vices that were dragging him down. Which side was victorious in that contest was concealed from our eyewitness, and is no more plain to us than to the one who saw it all and then came back to life. Still, it is certain that even though Stephen had been to hell and back, as we related above, he did not completely correct his life. Consequently, when he went out of his body many years later, he still had to face a life-and-death battle.

Conclusion

Right after *Life After Life* was published it was obvious that this was such an enormously popular subject that my life would never be the same. I quickly realized that death is our greatest mystery and everyone is interested in solving it.

NDEs intrigue us because they are the most tangible proof of spiritual existence that can be found. They are truly the light at the end of the tunnel.

CHAPTER 5

Why the NDE Isn't
Mental Illness

At the end of one of Dr. Michael Sabom's lectures, an irate cardiologist stood up and confronted the noted NDE researcher. He had been a doctor for thirty years, he declared, during which time he had brought hundreds of people back from the brink of death.

"I've been in the middle of this stuff for years," he said angrily. "And I've never talked to a patient who had one of these near-death experiences."

Before Sabom could respond, a man behind the doctor stood up. "I'm one of the people you saved and I'll tell you right now, you're the last person I would ever tell about my near-death experience."

The message from that encounter was clear: many doctors and medical personnel aren't sympathetic to NDEers because they don't know how to cope with nor are they receptive to them. Many of the NDEers I have talked to over the years told me that their doctors advised them to ignore their experience. At best they declared that the NDE was a bad dream, something to be forgotten. At worst, they implied that the experience was a form of mental illness that might have to be dealt with on the psychotherapist's couch or in a mental hospital. Never mind that the NDE was being talked about as a positive and uplifting experience. For many medical professionals, an NDE is a sign of insanity.

A far larger number of the NDEers I have talked to don't even bother to tell their doctors about the experience, nor many relatives and friends, for that matter. They are aware from the moment they return that they would be thought "crazy" if they told anyone about "the tunnel" or the "Being of Light." Hence, they keep this marvelous experience to themselves, never telling anyone about the event that has transformed them so completely. Sometimes, to tell anyone about the NDE invites a world of trouble.

This was the case for Martha Todd, a respected professor of English at a southern college. Several years ago, she had a very intense NDE while undergoing a routine surgery for removal of a cyst.

Almost immediately after the anesthetic was administered, an allergic reaction to it caused her heart to stop. She remembers hearing the physician shout for someone to bring the "crash cart," the equipment needed for emergency resuscitation. She says she was aware of being "in trouble," but at the same time "being so relaxed and at peace that I didn't care." She heard someone in the room say "cardiac arrest," and then it happened:

> *I found myself floating up toward the ceiling, I could see everyone around the bed very plainly, even my own body. I thought how odd it was that they were upset about my body. I was fine and I wanted them to know that, but there seemed to be no way to let them know. It was as though there were a veil or a screen between me and the others in the room.*

> *I became aware of an opening, if I can call it that. It appeared to be elongated and dark and I began to zoom through it. I was puzzled yet exhilarated. I came out of this tunnel into a realm of soft, brilliant love and light. The love was everywhere. It surrounded me and seemed to soak through into my very being. At some point I was shown, or saw, the events of my life. They were in a kind of vast panorama. All of this is really just indescribable. People I knew who had died were there with me in the light, a friend who had died in college, my grandfather, and a great aunt, among others. They were happy, beaming.*
>
> *I didn't want to go back, but I was told that I had to by a man in light. I was being told that I had not completed what I had to do in life.*
>
> *I came back into my body with a sudden lurch.*

Almost immediately after the experience, Martha knew that her life had changed, that new realities had opened to her and that she would never again be the same. She wanted to tell her family and friends—even her doctor—about the experience. But as she grappled for the right words to explain the episode, she realized an awful truth. Rather than seeing interest and delight on the faces of the people around her bed, she saw instead concern and fear.

"They thought I had gone off the deep end," said Martha. "My mother was very worried. She tried to lecture me at first. She tried to tell me that it was easy to get carried away with the Bible and that I had to keep a cool head. I tried to tell her that I wasn't talking about anything I had read or heard in church, but that this was something that had happened to me."

If her parents were bad, her doctor was worse.

"He told my parents that I was delirious and hallucinating. He wanted me to see a psychiatrist right away. They thought I had lost my mind and I was sent to a mental hospital for treatment. I just couldn't believe that this was happening to me."

I would like to think that events would be different if Martha Todd were to have an NDE today. For one thing, psychiatrists and psychologists now know about NDEs, so a person having one would probably not end up in a mental ward. But unfortunately, many doctors and their support staffs know little about the NDE and how it differs from mental illness. And since they are the first people an NDEer is likely to encounter after an episode, they can make a person feel ashamed of such a beautiful experience.

This is too bad because unlike mental illness, an NDE is likely to lead to mental adjustment and well-being that will make the person better adjusted than they were before the experience. Mental illness, on the other hand, leads to unhappiness, despair, depression, and hopelessness.

Even now, some medical professionals insist that NDEs are a form of mental illness. They do this because—in very superficial ways—the typical NDE resembles some forms of mental illness. I emphasize that NDEs resemble these problems in only superficial ways. When they are examined, as we will do here, you will see that mental illness no more resembles a near-death experience than a lamb resembles a lion.

The types of mental disturbances most often falsely linked to the NDE are (1) the major psychoses like schizophrenia and paranoia and (2) some organic brain problems like delirium, dementia, and a condition known as "temporal lobe epilepsy." Lets take a look at how these disorders get confused with NDEs and—more important—how they are nothing like them at all.

Schizophrenia-Related Psychosis

A psychosis—simply stated—is a condition in which people undergo a break with reality. They are no longer in touch with the world around them, for instance. This problem reveals itself in a number of symptoms:

- *Hallucinations:* Seeing people or things that don't exist.

- *Delusions:* False beliefs that a person can't be talked out of, like believing that one is Napoleon, for instance.

- *Loose associations:* A condition in which a person jumps from one unrelated thought to another in a disorganized and often indecipherable way.

Although there are a variety of psychoses, schizophrenia is probably the most widely known. It is a condition that involves "hearing voices" (auditory hallucinations), bizarre mannerisms, loose associations that often involve the use of bizarre, meaningless words and phrases called neologisms, and gradually worsening apathy.

In a schizophrenic episode, a person is likely to be tormented by voices and chaotic, fragmented thoughts that have such a debilitating effect on the personality that in many cases the overall course of the illness is downhill. Often, schizophrenics become isolated, unable to relate to anyone else in a meaningful way. In short, they become incapable of functioning in society.

Right away, you can see the difference between this terrible mental illness and the generally uplifting near-death experience. Although many NDEers hear voices during their episode, the voices are coherent words, not indecipherable gibberish.

Where schizophrenics are likely to "go downhill" in their ability to cope with society, NDEers are likely to function better in the world around them. And although NDEers may have seen a "Being of Light" during their experiences, they don't think they are Napoleon or God because of it. The NDE is a coherent experience that happens, is over, and has a positive effect on one's life. Schizophrenia is made up of incoherent experiences that can go on for long periods of time—maybe even an entire lifetime—and generally drag one down.

In my experience as a psychiatrist, the resemblance between the NDE and schizophrenia is superficial, and rapidly dissolves when one pays close attention to individual cases. To illustrate this I will quote from two interviews—the first with a schizophrenic and the second with a person who has undergone a near-death experience. Each interview is a typical example of its kind. These will certainly help you decide for yourself whether or not the NDEer should be considered mentally ill.

Schizophrenic

Here is a portion of an interview done in a mental hospital with a fifty-eight-year-old, chronic schizophrenic woman. The doctor was interviewing her to get a picture of what she had been through in her life and what was going on in her head.

Doctor: Hello. I would like to know what brings you to the hospital. Why did you come in?

Helen: I don't know why they brought me in here.

Doctor: Well, what kind of difficulties are you having today? Is there anything troubling you?

Helen: Well, I know that those people are putting radio waves in my head . . . on a frequency not of our world.

Doctor: What people are they?

Helen: I don't know who they are. They are at least a thousand miles away. But they are sending messages into my head all the time. Please call the FBI and get them down here. I know that they have ways of tracing where radio waves are coming from and this is getting terrible. They are broadcasting into my head all the time.

Doctor: Are they broadcasting now?

Helen: Yes, they are.

Doctor: Are you hearing them now?

Helen: Yes.

Doctor: So you are hearing voices now?

Helen: Yes.

Doctor: Can you tell me what the voices are saying?

Helen: Well, I can't tell exactly what they are saying.

Doctor: Are they men's voices or women's voices?

Helen: (Pausing for a few moments to listen and reflect.) I just don't know.

This brief segment of a much longer interview is very typical of how schizophrenics talk about the "voices" they hear. Most of the time, the patients can't hear what the voices are saying. They are distant or garbled. Sometimes the voices even sound like the rumbling of distant thunder. When they can understand the voices, they are usually saying hostile things to the patient or about the people around them.

It is clear from the way schizophrenics act that these hallucinations have an auditory quality. They frequently turn their heads when they hear the voices, even moving their eyes or ears in the direction of the "conversation."

NDEer

By way of contrast, consider the following excerpt from an interview with Alice, a sixty-year-old woman who had a classic NDE while being resuscitated from a cardiac arrest. In this interview, she described leaving her body and observing the resuscitation from above. Subsequently, she went through a tunnel into a brilliant light in which she encountered three deceased relatives, her mother and father, and a sister. Later, the interviewer asked her in detail about some of the features of her NDE.

> *Doctor:* Now, you said that when you were out of your body in the hospital room, you could see the people who were trying to get your heart started again and you could tell what they were saying.
> *Alice:* Yes, you could. But you couldn't get their attention. To them, it was like I wasn't there at all.
> *Doctor:* Well, what I want to know is, how could you tell what they were saying? I mean, did you hear their voices or was it more like . . .
> *Alice:* No, I didn't hear voices. No, it isn't like you hear their voices like I'm hearing you now. I don't remember hearing anything like that with my ears. No, you understand them without them having to say words. I could understand what my doctor was thinking. I felt how worried he was about me and he thought I was going to die.
>
> He was going to say, "You better call the family because she is going to die." I knew he was going to say it. It wasn't like hearing his voice at all. I don't think I could have heard his voice then, anyway. I was dead. I just picked up on what he was thinking.
> *Doctor:* Did your doctor tell someone to call your family? Do you know?

Alice: Yes, he did. I talked with my doctor a long time about this, and he didn't know what to think. He asked me to tell a lot of it over several times and he kept shaking his head. He said that all the things I said about what had happened were true, but he couldn't believe that I knew about them because he had thought I was dead at the time.

Doctor: So he did call your family, then? Or tell someone to?

Alice: Yes, he told me he did, just like I knew that he did. And other things, too, that I told him about and he said they were right.

Doctor: Yet you said it wasn't exactly like hearing?

Alice: That's right. More like reading their minds. I could see their mouths move to talk but I don't remember hearing their voices. It was more understanding. Just understanding what they were thinking.

The interviewer asked Alice for more detail on the part of her experience in which, after passing through a tunnel, she found herself in the presence of her mother, father, and sister, all of whom had died many years previously.

Doctor: Now it was also in this light that you felt you were with some of your relatives who had died.

Alice: Yes. My father, who had died in 1932, I think it was. My mother was there and she died in 1949. My sister died in about 1970.

Doctor: You felt you communicated with them in some way?

Alice: Oh yes. There was a lot of love. There was love both ways. You knew what was in their hearts. They also told me that I had to go back. They knew I wasn't supposed to be there yet. They said that I would have to go back and finish my life.

Doctor: Hmmm. Do you know what they meant by that?

Alice: No, I never have figured out why I wasn't allowed to stay over there. But I guess they were in a better position to know than I was. I still don't know why I had to come back.

Doctor: So you said they told you that you had to go back. Was that like hearing them?

Alice: No, doctor. Again, it's not like that. When you are over there you don't need words. You know immediately what's on their minds and they know about you too. I just can't express it better.

As you can see, there is a very real difference between a psychotic experience and an NDE. As I have already pointed out, the NDE tends to be a growth experience, one that leads to a greater degree of joy and fulfillment. Psychotic experiences tend to go just the other way, into depression and despair.

Furthermore, you can't say that persons undergoing NDEs are having hallucinations when they are having an out-of-body experience because hallucination implies that they are out of touch with the reality of their surroundings.

As you can see from Alice's experience, she was very aware of what was going on while she was "dead." Hers is not a rare case. Other researchers and I have found that NDEers who had out-of-body experiences were able to tell us what was going on in their surroundings even though they were effectively "out of the picture." And the NDEers' stories have been verified by independent observers like medical personnel and family members. Again and again, these observers have been astounded at the accuracy of NDEers reports about what happened.

Organic Mental Disorders

Most near-death experiences occur under conditions that deprive the brain of oxygen. Because the brain can react in peculiar ways when deprived of this vital gas, many people have suggested that NDEs are nothing more than a reaction of the brain under duress, or in a state commonly known as "delirium."

Delirium frequently accompanies many types of severe illness and involves an acute chemical imbalance in the brain that is usually reversible without any damage to a person's mental state.

Delirious persons are disoriented by their condition, and their awareness of the world around them is impaired. They often have nightmarish hallucinations involving animals or insects. Thoughts are often fragmented and disorganized and unable to be completed. Rarely can delirious persons concentrate well and, when not involved in conversation, they may lapse back into a hallucinatory state.

Delirious persons appear to be watching the hallucinations impersonally, as though they are unfolding at a distance on a movie screen. One patient, for instance, told me of watching a stampeding herd of horses cross a vast desert. Although he seemed to be in the middle of them, it was very much like watching the event on a theater screen.

After delirium has been resolved, patients usually retain only hazy memories of it and describe it in a patchy, piecemeal way. They do not describe it as having deep personal meaning or as being in itself a spiritual transformation.

Over the years I have interviewed dozens of delirious people, both while they were actively delirious and then later, after the delirium had ceased. The experience they relate is entirely different from that of the NDEer.

Victims of delirium do not report the common features of the NDE: out-of-body experiences, panoramic memory, intense and pervasive love, or any of the other traits. The delirious report what happens to them as though it were a fluke, a troubling aberration that they are glad to be finished with. They do not describe their experience as a spiritual turning point, a vision that has brought new meaning and joy into their lives. It is not described as something that provides moral guidance. In fact, delirium is rarely described as being more than just a "bad trip."

For example, a man in his late seventies who had accidentally received too large a dose of medication was brought into the emergency room of a hospital violently agitated and talking in a rambling and incoherent fashion. I had an opportunity to interview him as he lay strapped to an examination table to keep him from thrashing around and hurting himself.

As I talked with him, he appeared to be gazing into the distance. He then pointed straight ahead and told me to look at the beagles running down by the stream.

Two days later when he had returned to normal, he could remember nothing about his experience in the emergency room.

I have been called on various occasions to see patients who were actively delirious and hallucinating. One man with a high fever complained of seeing fish swim around his head. A young man who was being treated for severe burns was plagued by visions of babies being boiled in cauldrons. A woman in her mid-thirties who became seriously ill with an infection following minor surgery reported seeing coffins on an intensely green football field. None of the people I have talked to who have been plagued by delirium described it in the glowing terms of an NDE.

Autoscopic Hallucinations

There are a multitude of fascinating medical phenomena that the lay public never hears about. Autoscopic hallucinations are among those. I bring it up here because some skeptics have claimed that the out-of-body experience described by NDEers is nothing more than an autoscopic hallucination.

But there is really a great difference between the two. Autoscopic hallucination is a projection of one's own image into one's visual space. So a person "sees" himself in the way they would see another person. It is a rare experience connected with migraine headaches and epilepsy. In my experience—I have never seen this in the medical literature—it is also connected with strokes.

Generally, a person sees only his or her own torso. But occasionally, people report full-length views. Very often the image mimics the movements of the person having the autoscopic experience. It is usually described as being a transparent image and—for reasons that are totally baffling to me—the phenomenon usually happens at twilight.

President Lincoln reported having such an experience while in the White House. He was lying one night on a sofa and saw a full-length image of himself as if looking in a mirror. It is hard to say what a report like that from today's White House would do to the nation!

Aristotle is the first person I know of to record a case study of an autoscopic hallucination. He described a man who walked the streets of Athens and frequently saw himself in the crowd.

I witnessed one such case firsthand with a stroke victim I was admitting to a hospital. He told me that his first sign of illness came while he was at the head table during a testimonial dinner and began to feel a headache. He didn't think much about it until he looked up and saw *himself* coming into the room. He was dressed in a suit, with a little flower on his lapel, and he proceeded to sit down at one of the tables and enjoy himself.

This man thought he was in the Twilight Zone. And in a way he was. His stroke had triggered an autoscopic hallucination.

These phenomena exist and are widely reported. But they are very different from the out-of-body experiences that happen during NDEs.

In the typical out-of-body experience, or OBE, the person reports that he has a point of view outside of his physical body. *And* he is viewing his physical body from a distance. He does not view his body as being transparent, but rather solid as it is in real life.

The OBEer also reports a center of awareness that is outside his physical body.

In an autoscopic hallucination, awareness is still from inside one's physical body, just like your experience now, in reading this book.

The OBE point-of-view is different in other respects, too. For instance, OBEers frequently report that they roam around and are able to tell precisely what is going on in places that their physical body didn't occupy. Since the perspective in autoscopic hallucinations is from the physical body, this phenomenon doesn't allow the person to travel.

It absolutely fascinates me that the mind has functions like autoscopic hallucination built into it. I have no idea what purpose such things serve. But I can tell you that autoscopic hallucinations are not connected to near-death experience.

"Between You and God"

As I hope I've shown, there is little correlation between mental illness and the NDE. This belief is starting to be absorbed by the psychiatric community. Rather than treating NDEers as mentally ill, many psychiatrists and psychological counselors are beginning to help them integrate the experience into their lives so they can use it in a positive way rather than repress it.

A man I once met after a lecture provided me with an excellent example of helpful and inspiring intervention by a wise psychiatrist. This man, Charlie Hill, was in his late forties when he had a cardiac arrest following emergency surgery for a bleeding ulcer.

He had a very typical NDE, but since this was the early seventies, such episodes were not widely discussed. Hence, when he told the surgeon and his wife about the episode, they both thought he was mentally disturbed. Charlie was immediately sent to a psychiatrist.

The psychiatrist listened patiently while Charlie described the remarkable and wonderful vision he had experienced on the operating table. At the end of his narration, the psychiatrist was obviously moved. "Mr. Hill, you are not psychotic," he declared. "You have had a spiritual experience such as some of the great men of history have had. What happened is between you and God."

Who could ask for more understanding?

CHAPTER 6

The Near-Death
Researchers

Until *Life After Life* was published, there was almost no research in the area of near-death experiences. In fact, there was almost no professional interest in the subject.

Most doctors ignored these occurrences if they were told them by their patients. Sometimes they even thought their patients were "crazy" and recommended psychiatric or hospital care for people who had these episodes. Like many doctors today, the M.D.'s of just a decade ago had never heard of "otherworld" experiences. But even if they had bothered to check the medical literature on the subject, they would have found virtually nothing. At that time just a few case studies existed, but nothing that constituted clear advice on what to say or do.

Today it's different. Thanks to a handful of researchers who read *Life After Life* and became interested in NDEs, doctors have a wealth of research—both anecdotal and empirical—from which to learn about this common phenomenon.

Not only can they learn about the traits of NDEs, but they also can find ways to talk to patients about this marvelous yet puzzling experience by looking at the work of these brave researchers.

I call them brave because it takes courage to go where no one has gone before. Like the great explorers of the earth, these people explore the geography of the spirit. Some, like Dr. Michael Sabom and Kenneth Ring, do their exploration in very methodical ways to derive hard medical facts. Dr. Melvin Morse is after hard medical facts too, only from the near-death experiences of innocent young children. Others, like philosopher Michael Grosso, look at NDEs through the looking glass of philosophy to find the meaning of the experience and its link to other spiritual phenomena. At some time they all faced adversity ranging from peer ridicule to self-doubt. But they have pressed on with their research because they felt that nagging need to answer these spiritual questions.

The people I am focusing on here are some of the most active pioneers in this rich new field of research. There have, of course, been others. But these are the ones who have been the guiding light.

Dr. Melvin Morse

A *pediatrician in Seattle, Washington, Dr. Morse has led the way in the study of the NDEs of children. His research is especially important in near-death studies, since he is dealing with an "innocent" population, people who haven't been exposed to a great amount of religious or cultural training. When their experiences are the same as much older NDEers, they have special meaning.*

Dr. Morse has been interested in NDEs since he first stumbled onto them as a resident physician in an Idaho hospital. He has been researching them ever since.

"I was skeptical for a long time," said Dr. Morse, when I

visited him at home in Seattle. "Then one day I read a long article in a medical journal that tried to explain NDEs as being various tricks of the brain. By then I had studied NDEs extensively and none of the explanations that this researcher listed made sense. It was finally clear to me that he had missed the most obvious explanation of all—NDEs are real. He had missed the possibility that the soul really does travel."

Here, in his own words, is Dr. Melvin Morse's story:

I first became interested in the near-death experiences of children when I was a resident physician in a Pocatello, Idaho, hospital. I was on call when a child who was a near-drowning victim came in. What an amazing case she was.

She was swimming in a YMCA pool on a very crowded day in one of these mob scenes. When everyone got out of the pool, she was still lying on the bottom.

A physician happened to be there. He was the kind of guy who had all kinds of medications in his gym bag, so he was able to start resuscitating her right on the scene. She was taken over to the community hospital and they called me in and asked me to see her.

She was profoundly comatose: fixed and dilated pupils, no gag, no corneas. I thought she was probably a goner, but I had to give her a CAT scan to see how bad she really was. To do that I had to put a tube in her vein so I could inject dye and get a good picture of her brain. I'll never forget the scene of putting that tube into her body. There was blood spurting all over while her parents and extended family circled us in a prayer ring.

There was no question in my mind that she would be severely brain damaged. I was wrong. She made a full recovery within three days.

Now, when I went to medical school, I was always told

you should ask open-ended questions. You should never ask a question they can answer with a "yes" or "no." That is the bane of my practice. My partner sees fifty patients a day. But I can't see that many because I get too gabby and I want to hear the whole story.

Anyway, I saw this little girl for follow-up after she was discharged from the hospital. I said to her, "Tell me what happened when you were in the swimming pool." What I wanted to know was if she had a seizure, if someone hit her on the head, or what. Instead, she said to me, "You mean when I went and sat on the Heavenly Father's lap?"

Whoa, I thought. "That sounds interesting," I said. "Tell me about that." Needless to say, I was taken aback by what I heard.

What this seven-year-old told me was so detailed it was amazing. She said she was in a dark place, she didn't know where she was or how she got there. She couldn't talk. It was obviously some kind of tunnel. Then this woman came to greet her. She had long, golden hair and was named Elizabeth. She took her by the hand, then the tunnel became even darker, and the little girl found she could walk. They walked together to a place she perceived to be heaven.

She told me the place she went to had a border. It seemed to be a circle which she couldn't see beyond because the border around it was filled with flowers.

I just wanted to do a reality test on her, so I asked: "What does it mean to die?" And she said to me: "You'll see. Heaven is fun." I have never forgotten that because she said it with such confidence; looking me right in the eye she said, "You'll see."

But then I asked her again, "What does it mean to die?" And she said, "Well, what happened to me really was not dying because when you die you are under the ground in a box."

I asked her if this experience was a dream. She said, "No, this is something that really happened to me. But it wasn't death. Death is when you are put in a box under the ground."

This was so perfect because it fits into a seven-year-old's perception of death.

Then she said she met Jesus who took her to the Heavenly Father. The Heavenly Father said something like: "You're not really meant to be here. Do you want to stay here or do you want to go back?" She answered that she wanted to stay. Then he asked her a different way. "Wouldn't you like to be with your mother?" To that she said yes, and then she woke up.

When she awoke, she asked the nurses for her friends. Those were the first words she spoke. She said, "Where's this guy and that guy?" These were the people she had met up in heaven. And of course, the people at the hospital didn't know what she was talking about.

I talked to those nurses and they absolutely confirmed that. They said when she woke up she started asking about people who weren't related to her and that no one seemed to know anything about. And then she lapsed back into unconsciousness again and that memory had completely faded. In fact she didn't discuss the episode further until I saw her at the follow-up.

It was such a vivid experience that I became intensely interested. I decided I would write this up for medical literature since there wasn't such a description of something happening to a child her age. I quizzed other families whose children had experienced NDEs about their belief systems and I asked what their death teachings were. I really tried to see whether this was cultural.

Sure enough, virtually none of it was cultural. It seems cultural on the superficial level but when you really probe and ask what she was taught about death and the hereafter, it was nothing like this experience.

She was told that death was like a sailboat. That when you die you get in a little sailboat and you're across the sea to another land. Certainly there was no concept of guardian angels, or people taking you to heaven or having decisions to go back to earth or stay. Virtually none of her experience had any resemblance to the death teachings of her family.

Still, many of my colleagues insisted this must be a cultural experience, one related to her deeply religious family. I decided I would study that for myself.

I worked for an outfit in Idaho called Airlift Northwest, which is an air transport to the hospital. This gave me the opportunity to be involved with dozens and dozens of resuscitated children as a part of my daily life.

I asked the head of the Airlift program if I could study NDEs in an informal way. He said it was fine, so I interviewed every child survivor of cardiac arrest at this hospital over a ten-year period. My study took about three years and sent me back through hundreds of records.

No one over the age of eighteen was allowed in the study at all. I interviewed every survivor of a cardiac arrest, everybody who had a Glascow Coma Score of four or less, and everybody with some kind of disease process that they would likely die from.

During this time I also read everything I could find about transient depersonalization (TD), which is the theory that the mind plays tricks on itself when faced with a terrible situation. I did this because one of the doctors said that it would account for the NDEs. I read case histories of TD and didn't think it sounded like near-death experiences at all.

Then I went through every drug that my patients could be on. And I read case histories of what it could be like to be on those various medications. They didn't seem anything like an NDE to me. But I wanted to see for myself, as well.

So in my patient population, I had a whole bunch of patients who were not near death but who I thought had particularly scary disease processes. If anyone should have an NDE for any of these other reasons—narcotics, drugs, transient depersonalization—they would be the ones.

I deliberately picked some very bad cases. I had one patient who had been paralyzed from head to toe for four months. She had pain so bad that she was on every narcotic and mind-altering drug you could imagine, including Thorazine, Valium, Demerol, morphine, morphine drips. Then she was also being treated with active, on-going hypnosis in which she actively visualized herself out of her body. There was no better case control than that. I mean, if she doesn't have a sort of near-death experience from transient depersonalization, nobody would.

Well, she didn't. Nobody in the control group had any experiences like NDEs. They didn't have any experiences at all. They all said the same thing: "I had dreams of doctors coming at me with syringes." Or "I had monster dreams." But none had what we know as NDEs.

The other group—the people who had been very close to death—all had NDEs. Every one of them. They went down tunnels, viewed their bodies from outside of themselves, saw beings of light. All of them had virtually identical experiences.

One way or another there was always a light in their cases. One fascinating patient actually luminesced—glowed—according to her father. He had to free-dive forty feet deep in Puget Sound to save her. He said he was able to find her only because she was bathed in this white light.

Another patient told me that he didn't see a light or a tunnel—he saw his own body lit up with light. He was in a world of darkness up in the corner and he looked down and saw his own body bathed in an illumination of soft white light. Then he got sucked back into his body when they shocked him with the paddles. No real emotions. No real feeling. It wasn't happy or sad. It just happened.

Most of the kids in the study didn't think this was the most powerful event in their lives, which to me was very realistic. They took it as a matter of course: this is what happens when you die.

I've concluded a couple of things from my work with children:

- I know this sounds very unscientific, but I am convinced that virtually every person who has had cardiac resuscitation has had some kind of NDE episode, be it out-of-body or going all the way to the being of light. The only reason they don't remember them is that perhaps the drugs they are given—Valium, for example—cause amnesia. I've come to this conclusion because the patients in my study who had fewer drugs had the most powerful experiences. It makes sense, if you think about it. After all, the patients who are in a morphine fog are less likely to remember an experience than the ones who have less medication to interfere with memory.

- We are taught in medical school to find the simplest explanation for medical problems. After looking at all the other explanations for near-death experiences, I think the simplest explanation is that NDEs are actually glimpses into the world beyond. Why not? I've read all the convoluted psychological and physiological explanations for NDEs, and none of them seem very satisfying.

Who knows—who really knows—maybe the souls of NDEers really do leave their physical bodies and travel to another realm.

I've looked at all the evidence and I can't see why not.

Dr. Michael Sabom

Dr. Michael Sabom was a skeptic when he first heard of near-death experiences. But as his interest in the subject grew, Sabom decided to perform a study that has become a benchmark in the field of near-death research. He examined the NDEs of 116 people, dividing their experiences into three types: autoscopic (leaving the body), transcendental (entering a "spiritual realm"), and mixed experience, in which the person has both autoscopic and transcendental traits.

Perhaps the most interesting aspect of Sabom's research is his close evaluation of the out-of-body experience. In such an experience, a person claims to leave his body and watch his own resuscitation as the doctors performed it in the emergency room or during surgery. Sabom had thirty-two such patients in his study.

He compared their descriptions of the resuscitation procedures with those "educated guesses" of twenty-five medically savvy patients about what happens when a doctor tries to get the heart started again. He wanted to see what the average "medically smart" patient knows as compared to someone who had an out-of-body experience.

He found that twenty-three of the twenty-five people in the control group made major mistakes in describing the resuscitation procedures. On the other hand, none of the near-death patients made mistakes in describing what went on in their resuscitations—strong evidence that these people were actually outside their bodies looking down.

I spoke to Sabom in Atlanta, where he is now a cardiologist in private practice. "I am a strong Christian and see the afterlife as one of the basic Christian beliefs," said Sabom. "I don't think this stuff should be sensationalized like it has in

*some instances, but looked at as part of the normal living and
dying processes. If people would look at NDEs in that light, it
might not seem so weird."*

Here, in his own words, is how his interest in NDEs began
and snowballed into a major study and his book, Recollections of Death: A Medical Investigation.

In 1978, I was in Gainsville, Florida, and I heard about
the book *Life After Life* from Sarah Kreutziger, a psychiatric
social worker, who presented it in Sunday school class. After-
wards, she asked me what I thought about it and I told her I
thought it was ridiculous. I had never heard of these experiences from my own patients. I even went to the hospital and
asked other physicians if they had heard of them, and they
had not.

Still, she had challenged me to read the book and I did. I
thought it was very entertaining, but quite frankly didn't
think there was much factual substance to it.

She was asked to present the book to the church in general
and we figured it would be interesting to do it together. But
to do that, we decided we should try to find a few patients
who'd had the experience. I casually asked several of my
patients and was amazed at the great number who had
experienced it. I was further amazed that these experiences
were happening right under our noses to people we were
taking care of and we didn't even know about it.

We became so intrigued with the subject that we decided
to do a study on NDEs. We began interviewing people who'd
had cardiac arrest or other near-death events to see what
percentage had NDEs, the types of people, under what circumstances, etc.

We interviewed about 120 people in a study that continued for about five years. That formed the nucleus for the book
I wrote.

You should know that I came at this subject from a highly skeptical standpoint. My background is very traditional. This was really the first time I had become involved in anything offbeat from the traditional medical education.

Studying NDEs was a process of breaking down some preconceived notions. After all, through my education I had focused on the physical aspect of man, not the spiritual.

The aspect of the experience I became most interested in was the autoscopic, or out-of-body, experience. People who experienced this actually seemed to be able to accurately see what was going on in some type of paranormal way.

The case that brought it home to me was that of a Vietnam veteran currently working at the VA hospital here in Atlanta who had his experience on the battleground.

He was very badly wounded and had an out-of-body experience out in the field of combat. He watched his physical body as the Vietcong came onto the battlefield, stripped him of everything he had—his watch, his gun, even his shoes.

He watched that from above and then continued to watch as the Americans came back through later that afternoon and put his body in a black bag and stacked it on a truck for the journey to the morgue where they were going to embalm him.

Well, the embalmer made an incision over the left femoral vein to inject embalming fluid and noticed that there was excessive oozing of blood.

Doctors were brought in and determined that he was still alive. They checked him over and took him right away to the operating room, where he had his arm amputated.

He watched all of this.

I'd heard that he had been injured over in Vietnam but I had not heard he'd had an experience like this. I was just talking to him about Vietnam when he told me about this experience.

I believed him on a certain level, but as a scientist I wanted some kind of proof. "Would you mind if I looked at your left groin," I asked. I did, and there was a little scar about an inch long right over his left femoral vein. To me, that really brought home the fact that this fantastic story this guy had told me was true.

Several people actually thought he was dead there on the battlefield. But he was still conscious in another realm. His demeanor when he was in this situation was calm and peaceful. He was not horrified or going through a lot of pain and suffering. I find that very comforting. I also think about that when I treat coma patients. Are they watching me from somewhere?

Anyway, the Vietnam veteran was convincing, but I can't tell you at what point I believed that this was really occurring. It took a lot of people with NDEs. But when they all started telling basically the same story, I began looking into whether they had heard about or read about it or whether they had access to somebody else's experience after resuscitation.

The first thing that went through my mind with these people was, "You have read Raymond Moody's book, haven't you?" And the patients hadn't. Most of these people were from north Florida. They were not tuned into the media and stuff like that. They rarely read books and only occasionally read a newspaper. But the experiences were so similar that I had the feeling that they were telling me an experience that came right out of a movie.

During my research I heard of several instances of somebody dying and somebody else being aware of it at that very moment. I didn't include these in my book because I didn't think this telepathy was really linked to NDEs. Now I'm not so sure. The more I hear of this, the more I think it might be some sort of out-of-body experience.

One very remarkable instance happened with a six-year-old boy who was dying. He was being given morphine intra-venously, but after his first of three visions, he no longer needed the morphine because he was feeling no pain.

During his first vision he saw a white horse and a heavenly sphere that he went to. There he talked to God.

During his second vision, he telepathically contacted his grandmother, who had been bedridden for many years because of severe arthritis. I know this happened because the boy was undergoing the vision at four A.M., the same time the old woman awoke and insisted that her caretaker deliver her to the child's bedside at the hospital. When she arrived he was in the throes of his third vision and was virtually incoherent. He died shortly thereafter.

I know this sounds like something out of the *National Enquirer*, but this story, and others like it, have been verified.

After a while, the facts became so overwhelming that I could not deny the reality of the NDE. Still today, when I think about it in a traditional fashion, I just think I made something out of nothing. Then I'll start reading some of the interviews I had with some of these people and realize once again that there really is something here.

Unfortunately, that feeling isn't shared by many of the people who control the world of medical publishing, where there is negativism toward the NDE because it is something that is a little offbeat.

It's too bad that these medical editors won't allow us to reach more doctors with information about NDEs, especially in this age of high technology when so many people are surviving medical calamities that used to kill them. Now what was once classified as "deathbed visions" has become an NDE for a patient who needs to be counseled about this remarkable experience. If doctors don't know what these things are all about, the patient is being short-changed.

Michael Grosso

Dr. Michael Grosso is a philosopher, and because of that he occupies a unique place among NDE researchers. Rather than compiling empirical data like his more scientific counterparts, Dr. Grosso searches for links between near-death experiences and the great philosophical truths. He finds them, too. As you will see here, Dr. Grosso finds strong connections between the experiences of NDEers he talks to and the teachings of great philosophers from Plato to Christ.

But he has found other connections as well. When I talked to this Columbia-University-trained philosopher at his home in Riverdale, New York, I was intrigued to hear his belief that NDEs are linked to many other parapsychological phenomena, like channeling. "There are many doors into the spiritual realm," said Dr. Grosso. "And most of them are easier than almost dying."

To Dr. Grosso, the NDE is a glimpse at nondenominational religion, "religion the way God intended it." Here are his own words on the subject.

There is this wonderful myth in Plato called "The Myth of the True Earth." It is told by Socrates from prison, where he is about to drink poison as his fatal punishment for "corrupting" the youth of Athens.

He is talking to his followers about the state of the "true earth" and the spirit as it is freed from the body.

In this myth he says:

> But those who are judged to have lived a life of surpassing holiness—these are they who are released and set free from confinement in these regions of the earth, and passing

*upward to their pure abode, making their dwelling upon
the earth's surface. And of these such as have purified
themselves sufficiently by philosophy live thereafter altogether
without bodies, and reach habitations even more beautiful,
which is not easy to portray.*

The very interesting point Plato makes is that in this
higher modality on the true earth, human beings are in
direct communication with the gods.

That has been my experience with NDEers. I believe that
they have communicated with "the gods" as a result of their
experience. And because of this communication, we have a
lot to learn from them.

During the time that I was getting my Ph.D., I had a
number of extraordinary experiences. For one, I saw a UFO,
which sort of opened up my imagination.

Then I began to read in the world of parapsychology, and
then a few years later I stumbled upon the near-death studies. Suddenly, I found myself doing research on evidence of
life after death.

What particularly fascinated me about NDE was that it
sounded like people had taken a visit to the true earth that
Plato described. Moreover, these were real experiences, not
symbolic ones. People were having experiences in the twenti-
eth century that seemed to resonate with descriptions of
Plato's vision. That poked my fancy.

I began to seek out these people who'd had these experiences. I thought most of these folks wouldn't want to talk,
but I quickly found out that they were hungry for a receptive
ear. They would always qualify our discussion with the statement, "You know, I don't tell this to most people." Then
they would tell me these fascinating stories.

Most of the time I was excited. It was like hearing about a

journey into another country, one that I had been frightened about but know one day I had to explore myself.

For instance, one woman was having a very difficult childbirth, when suddenly her heart stopped. The doctors went to work on her immediately and vigorously while her husband—who was present—proceeded to panic. He was so distraught that the doctors practically considered him a second patient in the operating room.

Anyway, they got her going again and delivered the baby by cesarian section.

Later that night, she told her husband that she had left her body and witnessed from the ceiling everything that happened while she was near death. Although she was still groggy, she recounted what she saw, right down to his grieving form in the corner of the room.

Another NDEer described in vivid terms his powerful experience, one that ranged from an out-of-body experience right on through to a life review.

But the NDE didn't impress him as much as did the aftereffects. He was amazed at his increased sensitivity. He had been hard driven and logic bound before the experience. Now he found himself much softer and more imaginative.

My reaction most of the time was intellectual in the sense that I saw connections with all kinds of things. For example, I saw connections with *The Tibetan Book of the Dead*, I saw connections with St. Paul's experience in the Bible. Hearing these tales, I was filled with reminiscences of my education.

For example, there is a wonderful story of St. Thomas Aquinas, the eleventh century philosopher and theologian, who wrote voluminously almost until the end of his life. Then he had a vision of the light, after which he said, "All I have written is like straw." He stopped writing and within a year he quietly and mysteriously died.

After I listened to all of these stories, I felt I was getting from ordinary, untrained, unphilosophically and unmystically aware people a glimpse into a realm of being that I had only heard about from other sources like mystics, philosophers, and poets. In a sense these were more pieces of the jigsaw puzzle: it was the excitement of a picture that was coming into focus for me. That was the excitement that I had.

I sometimes wonder if maybe what one of the great Hindu sages said is true. His idea was that just by being in the presence of a highly evolved being, the less evolved gets a shock of the spirit—kind of like a laying on of hands. I sometimes wonder if that is the attraction of listening to these tales, that by being in contact with these people we are experiencing a kind of influx of energy.

I think it is truly a divine energy, too. I believe, as do many others, that the NDE is an inlet into a divine dimension of human consciousness that is latent in all of us. Other researchers have either suggested or argued that there are other ways to make contact with this dimension of consciousness. So in a sense, if you use Plato's Teutonic model of knowledge—that knowledge is a recollection of things we already know—then this spiritual awareness is already latent in us.

So I wonder if the reason for this profound attraction to NDEs is that hearing about them triggers a memory deep within us. It is sort of like a homecoming. Accounts of NDEs are like echoes that resonate from somewhere inside ourselves so that we want to keep hearing stories that awaken us more fully to that awareness.

At the same time questions occurred to me. How do we account for these experiences? Are they illusions, fantasies? I suppose the experiences that impressed me most of all were the ones in which there was some kind of verifiable out-of-body experience. When these accounts are accurate, you can't dismiss them.

On the whole, NDEs are positive events that transform people in positive ways. However, there is the occasional negative NDE. I have always taken the negative experiences seriously and wondered why there weren't more of them. They usually have positive effects on people just as the heavenly experiences do, but they can be absolutely frightening when they occur.

Let me tell you a very striking case. There was a young man who attempted to commit suicide. He had been a n'er-do-well all his life and wasn't really amounting to much. He took some kind of drug overdose and went into two different levels of experience. The first level was just physical pain and discomfort and horror as he sank into his near-death. He had a cardiac arrest in the presence of friends and turned blue.

Just by luck they were able to get medical personnel on the scene who resuscitated him. After he had entered into the critical death phase, he described to me the most nightmarish NDE that I had ever heard of.

He described images of some horrific beings clutching and clawing at him. It was something like descending into Dante's inferno. He had a claustrophobic, hostile, nightmarish NDE, without the slightest positive experience. No out-of-body episode, no being of light, nothing beautiful, nothing pleasant.

But this experience totally transformed him. He was a different person and I felt it. He had a clarity about him. He had a wholesomeness and a sense of self-determination. He was not an unusually gifted or ambitious person, but he had such a firm sense of where he was going in life that it was remarkable.

There is a very interesting twist on this story: I was delighted to have been able to tape-record his detailed account of his hellish NDE. But after he narrated the experience I tried to play it back on the tape recorder. The entire experience had been wiped out. The tape recorder that I had used for at least ten years had never failed me before and has never since. But when I tried to play back that experience, it was totally erased.

I have no explanation for it. A coincidence perhaps. Certainly a curious little footnote.

Studying NDEs has changed me in two ways. First, I feel more in touch with life. And that is a liberating effect. Another interesting change is that the near-death experience offers a glimpse into many things associated with religious experience.

Curiously, when I feel that I've had enough of this stuff, I find that it keeps coming back because it pertains to so many things in my life.

The religious aspects mean a lot to NDEers, too. It is a paradox that many people who have had an NDE can say that the best time of their life was when they were nearly dying. It reminds of Euripides, who said, "How do we know that the living are not dead and the dead living?" It suggests, you see, such a reversal of common sense. I find that attractive. Yet many people find that disturbing or distressing. I find something here almost surrealistic, and I have always been an admirer of the surrealists. In a sense, these experiences indicate to us that our normal obvious perception of the world may be in some way flawed.

There have been attempts to explain NDEs as a biological mechanism that kicks in when death approaches. I don't accept this explanation because I can't see what good it does for a human organism to have such an experience after the process of irreversible death has begun or has set in. I find it hard to imagine as a biological function because it is a paradox. What good would it do for the body to evolve that way?

Now spiritual evolution is another matter. As a philosopher once said, "Genius is what happens when your back is up against the wall." As a society, our backs are definitely against a wall—a nuclear wall. If you think about it, we aren't going to survive very long biologically at this point unless we do have a spiritual evolution—or de-evolution, since I think that what we are doing is getting back to the spiritual knowledge within us.

It may even be that in the hard-to-comprehend scheme of evolution the development of this self-destructing technology will actually stimulate spiritual awakening. Maybe spiritual evolution is what happens to us when, as a species, we are left no way out.

I think it's this risk of massive self-destruction through incredibly sophisticated weaponry that is forcing the global psychic phenomenon that seems to be taking place now.

The near-death experience is only one pattern in a family of patterns that have risen through this accelerated intellectual and technical development.

All these spiritual events have common threads. There are some interesting relationships between certain deep NDE and prophetic NDEs, for instance (see "The Flashforward" in Chapter 1). And there are links between some UFO contact cases and those amazing patterns of collective apparitional experiences called Marian visions, in which the Virgin Mary becomes visible on walls or other objects in towns.

I feel that there is some very fundamental interrelationship—that all of these experiences are manifestations of a collective transformation of consciousness that is taking place in response to possible nuclear annihilation.

It is interesting, by the way, that the UFO phenomena took off in 1947, within a few years of the first atom bomb. At the same time, there was a sudden worldwide acceleration of Marian visions.

I also believe the so-called channeling phenomenon, in which people are able to talk to the dead, is a version of the opening up process. In fact, you may say the channeling phenomenon is an easy way to the NDE, a non-life-threatening opening of the same realm of consciousness that is opened in the NDE. I think the people having all of these experiences are going through the same door, just in different ways.

This way of thinking has neither harmed nor helped my reputation among my colleagues. A few of my fellow profs at Jersey City State College where I teach have wanted to discuss these phenomena, but just as many have shown antagonism.

Academics tend to associate the study of these happenings with something retrograde, superstitious, and irrational. That attitude hasn't harmed me, but neither has it particularly helped me with my colleagues. I suppose I should be grateful for the polite neutrality.

Dr. Kenneth Ring

I have often said that it was Ken Ring who legitimized my work. Since my book relied upon the NDE "stories" of several dozen people from which I was able to discover certain patterns, it was largely criticized by the medical community. They felt I had approached the subject too much like a newspaper reporter and not enough like a scientist. Thankfully, Ring was there to take the scientific step.

He had been aware of NDEs as a psychology student. But it wasn't until reading Life After Life *in 1977 that he became intrigued enough to study the NDE.*

Ring examined in detail the experiences of 102 NDEers and was able to show that religion is no more a factor in the near-death experience than race. The same held true for a person's age. He also confirmed my findings that the NDE is ultimately a positive experience; the person who has it is transformed.

Ring's work is referred to by everyone who does meaningful NDE research. As you saw in Chapter 1, the method and questions he devised for his study have become the standard questions of NDE researchers. The results of his study are contained in his book, Life at Death: A Scientific Investigation of the Near-Death Experience. *Here is his story.*

I only had to hear of one near-death experience to hook me for life. That was in 1977, after I had read enough about this phenomenon to do some research. But that first experience was all I needed. I wanted to hear more and more.

The first story I heard was of a woman who had experienced a very rapid loss of blood pressure while in childbirth. During that experience, everything suddenly went black. When she "regained consciousness," she was up in the corner of the operating room looking down on the doctors as they worked to revive her and remove the child.

She didn't go down a tunnel or see any beings of light, but thoughts came into her head almost as though someone were talking to her. They told her that she would be all right and that she had to return to her body. "You've had a taste of this," the voice said. "Now you must go back."

The voice revealed to her that her baby should be named Peter (until then they had planned to name him Harold) and that he would have heart trouble that would be corrected in time.

This all proved to be the case, just as the voice had told her.

That story fascinated me. But I should say now that I wasn't always interested in near-death experiences. In my role as a psychologist, I was interested in altered states of consciousness, which is why I first read some medical journal articles on the subject. The experiences that I read about revealed what happens to people at the threshold of death. After that I read a couple of books on parapsychology and then *Life After Life*. I was hooked. I remember having a very electric feeling as I sat in my backyard reading. I even began scribbling ideas for research projects in the margins. My immediate feeling was, "This is what I want to do."

I decided to do a project of my own that would answer some of my questions about this experience:

- How many people experienced the five general stages of the NDE (feeling of peace, bodily separation, entering the darkness, seeing the light, entering the light).

- Does religion have an effect on the NDE?

- What were the aftereffects of the NDE? Did they really make people less fearful of death and more accepting of life?

I wanted to answer these questions, but first I had to find NDEers. To do that I went to a number of Connecticut hospitals and gave presentations to various committees to familiarize the staff with what I wanted to do.

It took a lot of talking to convince the hard medical types at these hospitals that my research was legitimate. But I finally got permission to do the work I needed to do. I even received referrals from the hospitals for people who had been close to death or clinically dead. I then went to their doctors to get authorization to speak to them.

It didn't matter to me if they had an NDE or not, since one of the purposes of the study was to find out how many people who come close to death have one of these experiences. But in reality, I was hoping many of the people had them because I wanted to hear about another NDE.

Well, the second person I talked to was an NDEer.

I was so excited that I felt like I was sitting on dynamite. And it continued like that—and does to this day—no matter how many of these people I listen to.

Typically, I would drive somewhere in New England to interview someone who'd had an NDE. The person was out of the hospital by then, so I would sit down in his or her living room and do the interview. Then I would drive back to Hartford, listening to the tape of the interview all the way back. I was so thrilled to hear these accounts that I listened to them again and again.

I won't go so far as to say that I was having a religious experience hearing these stories, but I will say that being around NDEers gives you a certain "hit." Do you know that feeling you get when you talk to someone who has traveled to a distant land that you've always been curious about? Or how you might feel if you were around an astronaut or some other explorer? It is a feeling like that, sort of like being in touch with a higher spiritual order.

The funny thing is that the people I talked to appreciated the interviews as much as I did. Many of them had never talked with anyone about these experiences or had done so with hesitation because they just needed to get it off their chests. Usually, they were misunderstood, and sometimes they were actually ridiculed.

To find someone like me who was genuinely interested in

their NDE was a great load off their mind. They could confide in me and know that I understood. They often had as many questions for me as I did for them.

Some of the people wanted to know if they were "special." Others wanted to know if they were "crazy." There were questions about why they felt so different after the NDE and why their families couldn't appreciate the experience. In almost all of the cases I've listened to, they just wanted to talk to somebody who understood but didn't judge. For them I was someone who was open and didn't want to put a frame around their experience.

In almost every instance, they would say: "This is the most profound, most secret, spiritual experience I have ever had." They would tell me that and I believed it. I could see from the look in their eyes that words alone could contain maybe one one-thousandth of the experience. There was certainly a sense of something private and holy being shared.

I had feelings of excitement that made it difficult to stay with the scheduled interview questions. Sometimes I chided myself for getting so emotional until I realized that by talking to these people, I was connected to a source of spiritual insight. Unless I was some kind of stone, I had to open up.

For instance, here's a transcript of the description of a very powerful NDE of a woman who almost died undergoing intestinal surgery:

> *I remember being above the bed—I was not in the bed anymore—looking down on me lying in the bed, and I remember saying to myself, "I don't want you to cut down on me." . . . I know that the doctors worked on me for many hours. And I remember being first above my body and then I remember being in, like a valley. And this valley reminded me of what I think of as the valley of the shadow of death. I also remember it being a very pretty valley. Very*

pleasant. And I felt very calm at that point. I met a person in this valley. And this person—I realized it later on—was my [deceased] grandfather, who I had never met. I remember my grandfather saying to me, "Helen, don't give up. You're still needed. I'm not ready for you yet." It was that kind of thing. And then I remember music. It was kind of like church music, in a sense. Spiritual music. It had a sad quality about it. A very awesome quality to it.

I've heard thousands of these stories, but I've never been able to "turn off" to them. People will come up to me and say, "I know you've heard all the stories you need to, but here's one more." And I'm right back with that same excited feeling. It's not an addiction, but it's certainly something you never get tired of.

I feel so intimate with these people that I do something psychologists aren't supposed to do with their clients. I call them "friends" In fact, I have remained in touch with several of the people I interviewed for the study.

I think this happened because we shared something that few people understand. Doing that created a bond that transcended the usual relationship that exists between interviewer and interviewee. Plus, these people are quite pleasant to be around, so it seemed a shame to see them on only one occasion. Many times I ask them if they would like to come to one of my classes or if they would appear on a radio or television program.

Of course, the difficult thing is that it becomes very hard to do research on your friends.

Doing near-death experience research has changed my life in many ways. For one thing, I have become more "spiritual." Not religious, mind you, but spiritual. What's the difference? A wise man once said: "A religious person follows the teachings of his church, whereas the spiritual person follows the guidance of his soul."

Studying NDEs has made me believe this. If you examine them, the experience underlies many of the great religions of the world. What is the basic message that the NDEer comes away with? That knowledge and love are the most important things. It is the formal religions that have added all the dogma and doctrine.

Dealing with NDEs has also changed the way I feel about life after death. In fact, I never use that phrase anymore. Instead, I think there is only life. When the physical body no longer functions, the spirit leaves and goes on living.

NDEs have given me a good sense of what that separation of body and spirit will be like. They have convinced me that there is only life, and death is something we view from the outside.

My studies have also taught me not to fear the end as we know it. I look forward to whatever that adventure may be.

Robert Sullivan

"I am in the plastics business for a living," says Bob Sullivan. "But that's not who I am." An NDE researcher is part of who this Pennsylvania resident is. His specialty: combat NDEs.

Sullivan became interested in NDEs in the late seventies after hearing a lecture by Kenneth Ring.

"I was intrigued with the subject," said Bob. "I went up to Ring and asked him if there was any research on what happens to people in combat. He said there wasn't and suggested that I should do it. So I decided right then and there to become a researcher."

Sullivan had all the components it took to research the subject. Besides curiosity, he had a military background, having served in the regular Army in the sixties, and in the reserves for several years after that. In addition, he had studied psychology in college but took a reductionist view of the subject. "Everything to me was chemicals and electrical impulses," he said. In addition to working in the family business, Sullivan did crisis counseling at a local hospital, dealing with people who were threatening suicide.

"Spending all of this time as a counselor helped me in my dealings with NDEers," said Sullivan. "In the course of my research I ran across some truly amazing cases. And to get everything I was interested in, I had to really probe."

Now Sullivan is back in business as the president of a plastics company. But in his spare time—what little there is—he still lectures groups on the NDE phenomenon.

In the three years that I did NDE research, I talked to almost forty combat veterans who had NDEs. These ranged in intensity from full-blown episodes to feelings of peace and tranquility in seriously wounded soldiers. Overall, their experiences were the same as those of people outside of the intense experience of combat, which is just more proof that these things are cross cultural in every sense of the word.

One NDE happened to a fellow I'll call Tom. He stepped on a mine in Vietnam that literally blew his leg off. He had the total experience. He left his body, zipped up a tunnel, saw a being of light, and had a past life review. Then he was back there on the battlefield, with dirt hanging in the air and blood pouring out of his body.

Anyway, when the medics got to him, they were shocked. Here he was with a leg gone, and all he wanted to talk about while they were putting the tourniquet on was his trip up the tunnel.

These NDEers were amazing. But unlike "citizen" NDE accounts, some of them had unusual experiences related to combat.

For example, two individuals reported to me that they could see bullets coming at them in sufficient time to move. They said that the bullets seemed almost like baseballs to them, objects that were so visible that they could dodge them like a baseball player ducking a beanball.

A World War II veteran claimed that he experienced 360-degree vision while running away from a German machine gun nest. Not only could he see ahead as he ran, but he could see the gunners trying to draw a bead on him from behind. Another veteran claimed that he could predict with 100 percent accuracy who was going to be killed or injured before a conflict. When word got around that he had this ability, people would line up by his bunk every morning to see whose "number was up" on that day.

Just like the NDEers and their metaphysical episodes, these people didn't ask for these powers. They just had them. They were as unexplainable to them as they are to those of us who study them.

All of this says to me that every time we think we've opened a door of understanding on NDEs, we find several more doors to open. In this case, other parapsychological issues arise in the course of investigating NDEs. For them, and for NDEs, I have no explanation, only assumptions.

Almost everyone asks me what I think NDEs are. I ask myself the same question: Are they a glimpse of the world beyond, or just a peculiar mix of chemistry? My answer: I don't know.

When I first heard about them, I thought NDEs were the open door to the beyond. I pulled together everything I had ever learned about psychology, chemistry, philosophy, and religion and began looking at this as closely as I could. The problem was that every question raised twelve more questions. This eternal lack of answers has been my main frustration.

I have now concluded that maybe the true meaning of NDEs can't be determined. I do think that NDEs are a glimpse into another plane of reality. But is that life after life? I just don't know.

I do think NDEs give us an excuse to talk about death, which is a subject in which we are all deeply interested, even if it is on a subconscious level. It is the most positive way I know to discuss the subject.

I'll give you an example of that. The fellow I sold my business to several years ago was a straight, hard-nosed businessman.

After we signed the contracts, he took me to dinner and asked what I planned to do now that I was free of business concerns. I thought he would consider me crazy if I told him I was going to study NDEs, but I went ahead and did it anyway.

He was fascinated. He told me about his aunt, who had experienced an NDE, and we spent the evening in animated conversation about death. I thought later that it must have looked to other tables like we were talking about a baseball team or something. But we weren't. We were talking about death.

I have come to some irrefutable conclusions about people who have near-death experiences.

For one, I do think NDEers give off a special kind of energy. You can certainly feel it when you're around them.

One night, I had to drive through a snow storm to deliver a lecture on NDEs. I thought no one would show for this session because of the weather, but when I got there, fifty people were waiting.

I delivered my little session on NDEs and then opened it to questions. Several people in the audience had experienced NDEs, and they began telling their stories. The session went on for a couple of hours.

I must tell you that after it was over, I was positively high. It was as though I had taken drugs. Because of the energy these people shared, I was up most of the night.

Since then, I call this "the group aura experience." Several people I know have had it. It is certainly the energy we receive from these people that makes the NDE researchers almost addicted to their subjects.

Another conclusion I've come to is that NDEs are ultimately positive experiences, even with war-ravaged veterans. This is important in light of the posttraumatic stress that many combat veterans experience. Although many of the NDEers I have spoken to have experienced postcombat stress, they have ultimately learned to understand the NDE in light of their other experiences and become better people as a result.

CHAPTER 7

Explanations

There are many attempts to explain near-death experiences as something other than spiritual events or glimpses into the otherworld. I intend to present as many of these arguments as I can and offer my—and others'—points of view on them. But first, I want to discuss why I think NDEs are spiritual experiences.

As you'll see in this chapter, there are several theories—theological, medical, and psychological—that try to explain the near-death experience as physical or mental phenomena that have more to do with brain dysfunction than with an adventure of the spirit.

But there are a couple of things that present enormous difficulty to these researchers: How is it that the patients can give such elaborate and detailed accounts of resuscitations, explaining in their entirety what the doctors were doing to bring them back to life? How can so many people explain what was going on in other rooms of a hospital while their bodies were in the operating room being resuscitated?

To me, these are the most difficult points for the NDE

researchers to answer. In fact, so far they have been impossible to explain except with one answer: they really occurred.

Before presenting the wide variety of attempted explanations that exist about NDEs, let's look at some examples of these unexplainable events.

A forty-nine-year-old man had a heart attack so severe that after thirty-five minutes of vigorous resuscitation efforts, the doctor gave up and began filling out the death certificate. Then someone noticed a flicker of life, so the doctor continued his work with the paddles and breathing equipment and was able to restart the man's heart.

The next day, when he was more coherent, the patient was able to describe in great detail what went on in the emergency room. This surprised the doctor. But what astonished him even more was the patient's vivid description of the emergency room nurse who hurried into the room to assist the doctor.

He described her perfectly, right down to her wedge hairdo and her last name, Hawkes. He said that she rolled this cart down the hall with a machine that had what looked like two Ping-Pong paddles on it (an electroshocker that is basic resuscitation equipment).

When the doctor asked him how he knew the nurse's name and what she had been doing during his heart attack, he said that he had left his body and—while walking down the hall to see his wife—passed right through nurse Hawkes. He read the name tag as he went through her, and remembered it so he could thank her later.

I talked to the doctor at great length about this case. He was quite rattled by it. Being there, he said, was the only way the man could have recounted this with such complete accuracy.

On Long Island, a seventy-year-old woman who had been blind since the age of eighteen was able to describe in vivid detail what was happening around her as doctors resuscitated her after a heart attack.

Not only could she describe what the instruments used looked like, but she could even describe their colors.

The most amazing thing about this to me was that most of these instruments weren't even thought of over fifty years ago when she could last see. On top of all this, she was even able to tell the doctor that he was wearing a blue suit when he began the resuscitation.

Another amazing case that says NDEs are more than just tricks of the mind was relayed to me by a doctor in South Dakota.

Driving into the hospital one morning, he had rear-ended a car. It had been very upsetting to him. He was very worried that the people he had hit would claim neck injury and sue him for a large sum of money.

This accident left him distraught and was very much on his mind later that morning when he rushed to the emergency room to resuscitate a person who was having a cardiac arrest.

The next day, the man he had rescued told him a remarkable story: "While you were working on me, I left my body and watched you work."

The doctor began to ask questions about what the man had seen and was amazed at the accuracy of his description. In precise detail, he told the doctor how the instruments looked and even in what order they were used. He described the colors of the equipment, shapes, and even settings of dials on the machines.

But what finally convinced this young cardiologist that the man's experience was genuine was when he said, "Doctor, I could tell that you were worried about that accident. But there isn't any reason to be worried about things like that.

You give your time to other people. Nobody is going to hurt you."

Not only had this patient picked up on the physical details of his surroundings, he had also read the doctor's mind.

After a lecture to doctors at the U.S. Army base in Fort Dix, New Jersey, a man approached me and told about his remarkable NDE. I later confirmed it with his attending physicians.

I was terribly ill and near death with heart problems at the same time that my sister was near death in another part of the same hospital with a diabetic coma. I left my body and went into the corner of the room, where I watched them work on me down below.

Suddenly, I found myself in conversation with my sister, who was up there with me. I was very attached to her, and we were having a great conversation about what was going on down there when she began to move away from me.

I tried to go with her but she kept telling me to stay where I was. "It's not your time," she said. "You can't go with me because it's not your time." Then she just began to recede off into the distance through a tunnel while I was left there alone.

When I awoke, I told the doctors that my sister had died. He denied it, but at my insistence, he had a nurse check on it. She had in fact died, just as I knew she did.

These are only a few of the cases that prove to me that NDEs are more than just hallucinations or "bad dreams." There is no logical explanation for the experiences of these people. Although tunnel experiences and beings of light can easily be chalked off as mere "mind play," out-of-body experiences baffle even the most skeptical in the medical profession.

Now let's take a look at some of the theories about NDEs and why they don't really work as explanations of this phenomenon.

Carl Sagan: Birth as the Tunnel Experience

Carl Sagan, noted Cornell University scientist and astronomer, is among those who have tried to explain the tunnel experience as leftover memory from the experience of birth.

On the surface, the comparison makes sense. Everyone in the world experiences birth, which could explain why NDEs are the same whether they occur in a Buddhist or a Baptist culture.

Struggling down the birth canal and being pulled into a bright and colorful world by people who are glad to see you are things most of us have experienced.

It is no wonder that Sagan makes the connection between birth and death. In his bestselling book, *Broca's Brain: Reflections on the Romance of Science*, Sagan writes:

> *The only alternative, so far as I can see, is that every human being, without exception, has already shared an experience like that of those travelers who return from the land of death: the sensation of flight; the emergence from darkness into light; an experience in which, at least sometimes, a heroic figure can be dimly perceived, bathed in radiance and glory. There is only one common experience that matches this description. It is called birth.*

Sagan's theory might seem logical, until you do what Carl Becker did. This philosophy professor from Southern Illinois

University examined pediatric research to determine just how much a child knows at birth and can remember of the experience. His conclusion: Babies don't remember being born and don't have the facilities to retain the experience in the brain.

Here is Becker's point-by-point examination of the argument:

- Infant perception is too poor to see what is going on during birth. In Sagan's theory, the NDEer who is greeted by beings of light is merely reliving the experience of coming out of the birth canal and seeing the midwife, doctor, or father.

  But Becker points up the fallacy of this assumption by referring to extensive studies of infant perception that show that the infant mind is not yet developed enough to perceive much of anything.

  One study shows that newborns cannot distinguish figures. Other studies show that:

- Newborns show no response to light, unless there is at least a 70 percent contrast between light and dark.

- They rarely focus or fixate on an object and when they do, they can only examine a small segment of an object for a very short period of time.

- Newborns have "corner-scan focusing," which means that when they focus at all, it is on a close, highly contrasting portion of an object and not on the entire object.

- Half of all newborns can't coordinate their vision at all on objects an arm's length away. And no infant less than a month old can fully focus on an object five feet away.

- Infant eye movements are "rapid and disorganized," especially when crying. Speaking of which, their eyes are very frequently blurred by tears, *especially* at birth.

Another point supported by studies is that children have little memory for shapes or patterns. And since their brains are not well developed and have not yet been exposed to life outside the womb, they have little capacity for encoding what they see.

Even if it were true that the NDE is some kind of dramatic playback of the birth experience, I have to wonder if it would be replayed in such a positive context as the near-death experience is for the vast majority of people. After all, birth involves a great disruption of the unborn's universe. Babies are pushed out into a world where they are turned upside down, spanked, and cut with scissors to sever the umbilical cord.

If the NDE were a playback of the birth experience, as Sagan suggests, it would not likely be such a positive transformation for most.

One final note on Sagan's theory. The tunnel experience most often involves a rapid passage toward a light at the end of the tunnel. In the actual birth experience, a child's face is pressed against the walls of the birth canal. Infants are not looking up at an approaching light, as Sagan's theory suggests. They can see nothing as they are pushed toward their entrance into the world.

Carbon Dioxide Overload and the Tunnel Experience

The tunnel experience has been called by some "the gateway into the otherworld," and is generally described as the feeling you would have if you found yourself speeding through a tunnel toward an ever-growing dot of light at the end.

Some researchers feel that the tunnel experience in NDEs is caused by the brain's reaction to increased levels of carbon dioxide (CO_2) in the blood. This gas is a byproduct of the body's metabolism—oxygen is breathed in and air containing higher levels of CO_2 is breathed out. When a person stops breathing, because of a heart attack or severe trauma—the bloodstream's CO_2 level rises rapidly. When the level gets too high, tissues begin to die.

Because CO_2 inhalation was used in the fifties as a form of psychotherapy, it has been experienced by a number of patients and its symptoms are well known. There are case studies of this no longer used therapy that describe the experience as feeling like a trip down a tunnel or cone, or being surrounded by bright lights.

It hasn't been reported that CO_2 inhalation is accompanied by such things as beings of light and life reviews.

I could almost accept the belief that too much CO_2 causes the tunnel experience if it wasn't for some of Dr. Michael Sabom's research.

In one of his cases, the Atlanta cardiologist coincidentally measured the blood oxygen levels of a patient at the very moment his very powerful NDE was going on and found his oxygen level to be above normal.

This questions the theory of the tunnel experience as CO_2 overload. If anything, Sabom's case study shows the need for further research before coming to a conclusion.

Must NDEers Be Near Death?

Many skeptics have said that NDEs are caused by the body simply being under stress, or the person being very ill. Although they admit that NDEs happen to people who nearly die, they also think the same experience can be had by the seriously—but not life-threatened—ill.

To test this theory, Dr. Melvin Morse interviewed eleven

children, ages three through sixteen, who had survived brushes with death. They included youngsters who had been in comas and cardiac arrest victims. Seven of these children had elements of the near-death experience, including memories of being out of their body, entering darkness, being in a tunnel, and deciding to return to their body.

These eleven patients were compared with twenty-nine children the same age who had survived serious illnesses that had low mortality rates and didn't involve brushes with death. None of this group had memories of any elements of the NDE.

This led Morse and his fellow researchers to conclude that "regardless of the . . . cause of these unique experiences, it is clear that children who survive life-threatening events (have) NDEs."

What this shows is that the near-death experience is something that is specifically connected with being on the brink of death as opposed to just being sick.

The NDE as Hallucination

Some people postulate that NDEs are merely hallucinations, mental events brought on by stress, lack of oxygen, or in some cases, even drugs.

However, one of the strongest arguments against the NDE as hallucination is their occurrence in patients who have flat EEG's.

The electroencephalogram, or EEG, measures the brain's electrical activity. It records this activity by scribing a line on a continuous strip of paper. This line goes up and down in response to the brain's electrical activity when a person thinks, speaks, dreams, and does virtually anything else. If the brain is dead, the EEG reading is a flat line, which implies that the brain is incapable of thought or action. A flat EEG is now the legal definition of death in many states.

For anything to happen in the brain, there must be electrical activity. Even hallucinations measure on the EEG.

But there are many cases in which people with flat EEGs have had near-death experiences. They, of course, lived to tell about them. The sheer number of these cases tells me that in some people, NDEs have happened when they were technically dead. Had these been hallucinations, they would have shown up on the EEG.

I should say right here that EEGs are not always an exact measure of brain life. Believe it or not, there are recorded cases of EEG machines being attached to bowls of quivering Jell-O and recording brain wave patterns.

Of course, that doesn't mean that the Jell-O is alive! What it means is that the EEG is picking up interference (probably from radio waves) that is registering on the instrument. Some call this the ghost in the machine.

Sometimes, the brain can be alive at such a low level that the EEG doesn't register the activity. An example of such a case was given to me by a doctor at Duke University. He said that they had a little girl attached to an EEG who was showing no brain wave activity on the machine.

The doctors thought she was dead and wanted to remove her from the life support system but the family refused. They insisted there was going to be a miracle and they gathered around her bed for a week of prayer.

She came out of it. The doctor who told me this story said that she revived and had recently finished the first grade. He emphasized that she would have been dead had they relied upon the EEG. He discovered what many other doctors have discovered: brain activity can be going on at such a deep level in the brain that surface electrodes don't pick it up.

Religion Not Required

Some people mistakenly think that only the very religious have NDEs. Research has shown, however, that this isn't true. Researchers like Melvin Morse and others have found that the very religious are more likely to think of the being of light as God or Jesus and will most often call the place at the end of the tunnel heaven. But their religious background doesn't alter the core NDE experience. They still leave their bodies, have tunnel experiences, see beings of light, and have life reviews just like the nonreligious. It isn't until later that they put the experience into a religious context.

As a brief aside, I have found that there are generally two types of people who ask about religion and the NDE. One group is trying to prove something about their interpretation of scripture by someone's near-death experience. The other group wants to know if atheists become religious after an NDE. What they imply is that an experience reported by an atheist would be more valid and objective. Their assumption is that such a person brought no prior conceptions into his NDE.

I have found that the entire issue of "religious background" is enormously more complex than just having religion or not having it.

When you deal with this, you have to take more than just the conscious mind into consideration. You also have to consider unconscious factors, too, because they may be very different from what one feels on a conscious level.

I have found that even though some people may claim to be atheists, they have some background in religion. After all, can you imagine someone reaching the age of six or seven and having no concept of God at all? I can't. Even if his parents had overtly tried to shield him from religion, they would surely be bombarded with the same images that all of us are bombarded with, especially since things like television ministers and neighborhood churches are unavoidable. These images create the notion of God in everybody's mind.

When a person faces a crisis like death, it certainly makes any notions of religion emerge. Just as there are no atheists on the battlefield, I think there are none on the brink of death.

So in my opinion, there are unconscious predispositions to religious beliefs that even researchers can't measure during a post-NDE interview.

By and large though, the very religious come back from NDEs very nondenominational. They report that God is more interested in the spiritual aspects of religion than the dogmatic ones.

Why All NDEs Aren't the Same

Some people argue that if NDEs are truly glimpses into the spiritual realm, then all NDEers should have the same experience. They should all view their body from a third person perspective, float down a tunnel, meet long-dead relatives, see a magnificent being of light, and have a life review.

As it is, they don't have the same experiences. I have quoted several anecdotes and studies in previous chapters that show the variety of traits exhibited by NDEers. Some people just have out-of-body experiences, while others have full-blown NDEs that take them into the spirit realm.

A study I have yet to discuss was conducted at California State University, Northridge, by J. Timothy Green and Penelope Friedman. They conducted in-depth interviews with forty-one people who were clinically dead or near death as a result of accident, illness, or suicide. Out of this group, a total of fifty NDEs were reported. The stages of these experiences were recorded and compared with Kenneth Ring's more extensive study. Since Green and Friedman were using a smaller sample of people, the percentages experiencing the different stages are in some cases quite different from those in Ring's study. Keeping that in mind, here is their comparison:

STAGE	RING'S STUDY	GREEN AND FRIEDMAN'S STUDY
1. Core affective cluster (peace and tranquility	60%	70%
2. Out-of-body experience	37%	66%
3. Tunnel/dark area	23%	32%
4. Seeing the light	16%	62%
5. Entering the light	10%	18%

This study and its comparison to Ring's work reemphasizes the variety of experiences that occur within the NDE. Although the people in these studies had what we call near-death experiences, their traits differed. Some simply had out-of-body experiences, while others had tunnel experiences. Still others experienced full-blown NDEs.

But still the basic question remains: Shouldn't everybody who nearly dies have the same experience?

My answer to that is "No." Think of it this way. If ten people visited France, I doubt that any of them would have the same experience. Three of them might say that they saw this big building. Five might say they had wonderful food, and two of them might say that they floated down a river. Everybody who came back from France would have a slightly different story, although there would be areas of overlap.

Similarly, in NDEs, while overlapping traits are reported within a common framework, no two experiences are exactly alike.

The Final Bedtime Story

Some people think that NDEs are the mind's mechanism for coping with our worst reality—death. Their theory is that the grimness of the situation leads the mind to trick itself into a better situation. Here is a simplified version of their proposed chain of events:

- There are two ways of responding to danger. If you can physically do something to change the situation—like get out of the way of a speeding car, for instance—you do that. If there is nothing you can do to change the situation—say you are hit by that car—then the mind must go within itself to cope with the problem. It does this by disassociating from the situation, in some cases going so far as to create a fantasy world.

- Although this fantasy approach may seem like a passive way to cope with a problem like being hit by a car, it may be in your best interest; since this life-threatening situation is painful and immobilizing, you are in too much distress to take any physical measures against the pain.

- To conserve energy and keep the body functioning, the mind slips deeper into this comfortable fantasy. Not only does this allow you to focus on something other than the excruciating pain of being hit by a car, but it also lets the body relax somewhat so it can better deal with its internal problems.

- This realization is accomplished by the brain's own ability to manufacture chemicals. When in pain, it makes so-called brain opiates, or endorphins, which are about thirty times more powerful than morphine. You may have felt the relaxing effects of these after a session of strenuous exercise. They cause the delightful sensation known as the runner's high. But being hit by a car has caused the brain to manufacture far more of this substance than jogging does. And it has caused them to be manufactured very fast.

  The disassociation and the fantasy become much more intense. Very strange things begin to happen. You think you leave your body. Or maybe you find yourself flying down a tunnel at supersonic speeds toward a bright light. You might see dead grandparents or late aunts and uncles. A magnificent being of light might greet you and take you on a review of your life. Maybe you want to stay in this "heaven." But the being of light tells you that it's time to return.

  Within moments—you don't know how long, really—you feel as though you've been "sucked" back into your body.

- You come back to the real world a changed person. This mind-produced drug experience has changed you. It has made you look at the world in a different way. You may think that this episode, which you find out is called a near-death experience, is a glimpse into the afterlife. But some researchers just think you almost saw your last "bed-time story."

This is a neatly packaged theory in many ways. But it still doesn't explain NDEs. For one thing, I don't know of any research that links endorphins with hallucinations or any other kind of visual phenomena.

I do know, however, that long-distance runners and other endurance athletes produce an extraordinary amount of endorphins while they are training or competing. They frequently feel almost euphoric after sustained exertion, which is in keeping with how these neurotransmitters are supposed to affect a person.

But I know of no cases in which endurance athletes have reported traits of the NDE, unless they almost died during exercise.

This theory also doesn't explain the out-of-body experiences we've discussed in this book, in which people accurately describe objects and events from outside their body.

It's my guess that this argument derives its plausibility from the fact that endorphins do create a state of peace and great bliss. They are expected to, since they are the body's mechanism for dealing with pain. However, logically speaking, the argument can't be taken any further.

Wish Fulfillment

People unable to face their rapidly approaching death may deny it by creating a fantasy that they survive. This is a form of wish fulfillment. It's defensive in nature because it pretends to defend us from final annihilation.

The most obvious argument against the wish fulfillment explanation is that NDEers have basically the same experiences. If this was merely a wish fulfillment, people would more likely be having vivid recollections of that wonderful Labor Day picnic or dreams of being surrounded by a bevy of beautiful women than having tunnel experiences and life reviews.

The events associated with near death could not be just ordinary wish fulfillment. If they were, the NDE reports would be entirely different, with no common bonds.

Another difficulty with this explanation is that it doesn't fit the facts about what happens during an NDE. A psychological defense like wish fulfillment keeps your situation as it is, since the state of the psyche wants to be kept intact.

A near-death experience is quite different in that it is a breakthrough. Instead of keeping people as they are, it makes them face their lives in a way that they have never done before.

After NDEs, people face personal truth in a very profound way. And it makes them happy. Unlike the wish fulfillment known as daydreams, which provide temporary relief from the world around us, the NDE is a platform for lifelong change.

Jung's Collective Unconscious

The great psychotherapist Carl Jung noticed that many of the same myths and beliefs exist in different cultures, even though they are not connected to one another. For instance, the creation story is almost the same for Papago Indians as it is for the ancient Greeks.

Jung called the overall theory "collective unconscious" and the individual instances "archetypes." These are programmed responses of all human beings. One simple example of an archetype is "mother." Conveying that word in any culture will conjure up very similar meanings, a basic universality.

Although Jung himself had a near-death experience, he didn't relate NDEs to collective unconsciousness. But Jungian scholars relate NDEs to archetypes because the experience is cross-cultural (experienced by people regardless of their racial background), and contains essentially the same elements for men and women of all ages.

The typical archetype experience might go like this: A person has a dream that contains elements not present in his or her conscious experience but that are similar to elements found in mythology or ancient rites. These unexplained elements are the archetypes.

Some Jungian scholars believe that death and near death causes this archetype imagery to be summoned from the deep subconscious. This imagery is basically the same for all of mankind: tunnel experiences, beings of light, past life reviews, etc.

This is a difficult theory to refute, especially since it is just that, a theory. And, like the other theories presented here, it has a grain of truth. But the major problem I see with it is that it doesn't explain the out-of-body experiences. Until that is done, no theory holds together for me.

An Experience of Light

For years I have been trying to discover a physiological explanation for NDEs. And for years I have come up empty-handed.

It just seems to me that all the so-called explanations are incomplete or ill formed. For the most part, the people who have derived them are people who have never taken the trouble to talk with NDEers, look them in the face, and listen to their stories.

If they did, maybe they would come to the same conclusions that philosopher William James did in describing mysticism.

He said that this is an experience that is noetic. It is self-certifying because it is a form of knowledge. It is so personal as to be beyond words. And it is profoundly life-changing.

It is, pure and simple, an experience of light.

Conclusion

"The Unspeakably Glorious"

For more than twenty years I have been working on the cutting edge of NDE research. In the course of my studies, I have listened to thousands of people tell about their deeply personal journeys into . . . what? The world beyond? The heaven they learned about from their religion? A region of the brain that reveals itself only in times of desperation?

I have talked to almost every NDE researcher in the world about his or her work. I know that most of them believe in their hearts that NDEs are a glimpse of life after life. But as scientists and people of medicine, they still haven't come up with "scientific proof" that a part of us goes on living after our physical being is dead. This lack of proof keeps them from going public with their true feelings. But in the meantime, they keep trying to answer in a scientific way that perplexing question: What happens when we die?

I don't think science can ever answer that question. It can be pondered from almost every side, but the resulting answer will never be complete. Even if the near-death experience was duplicated in a laboratory setting, then what? Science would only hear more about a journey that it couldn't see.

Various researchers have suggested ways of examining NDEs more closely than ever before. Their suggestions are interesting for what they might yield, but unlikely to be carried out for reasons of medical ethics. Although it is okay to think about some of these techniques, actually applying them might violate a patient's privacy and safety.

When a physician is working with a patient who is about to die, obviously the most important thing is not to be conducting scientific research, but to get this person back to life.

I think it would give the wrong image if those of us who have been researching NDEs advocated research on human beings at this critical time in their lives. That would be an intrusion on one of the most private and ultimate moments in a person's life.

To interfere in any way with the clinical task at hand would be morally reprehensible. And besides, there is little research that could be done that would reveal more about NDEs than the fine research covered in this book.

But there is some research that might be interesting as well as unobtrusive. One researcher suggested that objects not ordinarily found in an emergency room—some odd-shaped medallions, perhaps—be placed on the stomachs of patients being resuscitated during a heart attack.

That way, if they truly did have an out-of-body experience, they would be able to identify the object as they looked down from the ceiling.

On the surface this may sound like a good idea. But think about it: Would you want a doctor fooling with odd-shaped medallions when he should really be using every effort at his disposal to save your life? I don't think I would.

Not only would such a procedure present the ethics problems already mentioned, it would introduce incredible insurance liability for both the doctor that performed (or attempted) the resuscitation and the hospital that allowed an experiment like this to go on.

Another suggestion, one that I find more reasonable, would be to put some fixed points in the rooms where these resuscitations take place that could be seen only from a vantage point near the ceiling. That way a person could prove out-of-body experiences by describing these references as they described their own resuscitation.

References that I think would work especially well would be large, brightly colored stickers placed on top of hanging light fixtures, so they would be impossible to miss if one was to hover above them.

A very peculiar method of research involving gorillas was suggested at one point. I will mention it here only because it illustrates the frustration we face in not being able to replicate the NDE in a clinical setting.

It has been mentioned that gorillas might be taught sign language and then ushered to the brink of death in a controlled setting by doctors who then would resuscitate them. When the primates recovered, they could be "questioned" about their experience by their sign language trainer.

I am against this idea. For one thing, it would constitute cruelty to animals. For another, there would be very little gain. Whether an NDE occurs in a controlled setting or out in real life, the experience is likely to be the same. Something like a tunnel experience or a three-dimensional life review can't be witnessed by anyone but the subject it is happening to in *any* situation. So why risk even a gorilla's life trying?

I think this is a somewhat fanatical suggestion and hardly deserves comment. But I bring it up here because it is the only conceivable way of doing an animal study on the near-death experience.

In the absence of firm scientific proof, people frequently ask me what I believe: Are NDEs evidence of life after life? My answer is "Yes."

There are several things about NDEs that make me feel so strongly. One of these is the verifiable out-of-body experiences that I mentioned in the previous chapter. What greater proof is needed that persons survive the death of their physical bodies than many examples of individuals leaving their bodies and witnessing attempts to save it?

Although these out-of-body experiences might be the most solid scientific reason to believe in life hereafter, the most impressive thing about NDEs to me is the enormous changes in personality that they bring about in people. That NDEs totally transform the people to whom they happen shows their reality and power.

After twenty-two years of looking at the near-death experience, I think there isn't enough scientific proof to show conclusively that there is life after death. But that means scientific proof.

Matters of the heart are different. They are open to judgments that don't require a strictly scientific view of the world. But with researchers like myself, they do call for educated analysis.

Based on such examination, I am convinced that NDEers do get a glimpse of the beyond, a brief passage into a whole other reality.

The psychotherapist C. G. Jung summed up my feeling on life after life in a letter he wrote in 1944. This letter is especially significant since Jung himself had an NDE during a heart attack just a few months before he wrote it:

What happens after death is so unspeakably glorious that our imaginations and our feelings do not suffice to form even an approximate conception of it. . . .

Sooner or later, the dead all become what we also are. But in this reality, we know little or nothing about that mode of being. And what shall we still know of this earth after death? The dissolution of our timebound form in eternity brings no loss of meaning. Rather, does the little finger know itself a member of the hand.

Bibliography

In addition to work cited throughout this book, the following research helped form my knowledge and opinion on the subject of near-death experience.

Raft, David, and Andresen, Jeffry, "Transformations in Self-Understanding After Near-Death Experiences." *Contemporary Psychoanalysis*, July 1986, Vol. 22, pp. 319–346.
Feeling and thoughts associated with near-death experiences are reviewed and the cases of two patients who showed a particular type of self-understanding following an NDE are used as examples. These subjects showed a keen interest in knowing more about themselves, were acutely sensitive to sensory stimuli, and sought to create experiences with the quality of reverie. The subjects showed a recovery of memories, an awareness of previously unrecognized thoughts and feeling in others, and a grieving of losses. Another case, that of a man who experienced a sense of complete self-knowledge and heightened activity following a cardiac arrest is also presented. The insight that can potentially be acquired in the NDE is discussed.

Gabbard, Glen, and Twemlow, Stuart, "An Overview of Altered Mind/Body Perception." *Bulletin of the Menninger Clinic*, July, 1986, Vol. 50, pp. 351–366.
Abstract: Describes the various forms of altered mind-body perception, such as out-of-body experiences, depersonalization, autoscopy, schizophrenic body boundary disturbances, and near-death experiences. Taken together, these experiences form a continuum ranging from integrating, life-changing experiences to highly pathological disorders. Treatment considerations are discussed, and it is emphasized that these states are distinguishable and require different interventions.

Kirshnan, V., "Near-Death Experiences: Evidence for Survival?" *Anabiosis*, Spring, 1986, Vol. 5, pp 21–38.
The author argues that out-of-body experiences and other elements of near-death experiences, along with the pleasant affect that accompanies them, are not conclusive evidence for survival after death.

Becker, Carl, "View from Tibet: NDEs and the Book of the Dead." *Anabiosis*, Spring, 1985, Vol. 5, pp. 3–20.
The author presents a Tibetan perspective on near-death experiences and life after death by discussing the beliefs of the Bon religion and Vajrayana Buddhism and the theories derived from *The Tibetan Book of the Dead*. Similarities to modern NDE reports are noted, including out-of-body experiences and life review and judgment.

Bauer, Martin, "Near-Death Experiences and Attitude Change." *Anabiosis*, Spring, 1985, Vol. 5, pp. 39–47.
The association between near-death experiences and subsequent attitude changes is explored by administering a life attitude profile questionnaire assessing seven categories of attitudes to twenty female and eight male thirty-one- to

seventy-five-year-olds who had had a self-defined NDE. The questionnaire was designed to determine whether an individual is living as he or she desires or whether the individual lacks meaning in his or her life, and the strength of an individual's belief in a meaningful existence.

Rodabough, Tillman, "Near-Death Experiences: An Examination of the Supporting Data and Alternative Explanations." *Death-Studies*, 1985, Vol. 9, pp. 95–113.
This article summarizes a model of R. A. Moody's "life after life" with a brief listing of its component parts. Explanations for similar near-death experiences are organized into three categories: metaphysical, physiological, and social psychological. It concludes that those who believe in a life after death will find neither contradiction nor support in studies of NDEs.

Pasricha, Satwant, and Stevenson, Ian, "Near-Death Experiences in India: A Preliminary Report." *Journal of Nervous and Mental Disease*, March, 1986, Vol. 175, pp. 165–170.
The authors report clinical features of sixteen cases of near-death experiences investigated in India. Following brief clinical descriptions of four such experiences, the authors describe and discuss features in which the Indian cases differ from a larger sample of American cases. These features typically include the perception of being brought to a messenger, who after consulting a list, determines that there has been a mistake and that the sick individual is not ready to die. It is suggested that, while some features appear to reflect the influence of culture-bound beliefs, these cultural representations could reflect actual differences in the manifestation of the concept of afterlife in different cultures.

Greyson, Bruce, "A Typology of Near-Death Experiences." *American Journal of Psychiatry*, August, 1985, Vol. 142, pp. 967–969.

The author administered the Near-Death Experience Scale to eighty-nine NDEers. The scale quantifies the cognitive, affective, paranormal, and transcendental components of the NDE. Cluster analysis revealed three factor clusters: transcendental, affective, and cognitive NDEs. Subjects reporting these three types of NDEs did not differ significantly on demographic variables or on the Marlowe–Crowne Social Desirability Scale. The type of NDE was not significantly correlated with the specific cause of the NDE. However, NDEs that were sudden and unanticipated were rarely associated with cognitive experiences but frequently with transcendental and affective ones. Results do not support K. Ring's invariance hypothesis that NDEs are essentially invariable from case to case and suggest that psychological set may influence the type of experience.

Straight, Steve, "A Wave Among Waves: Katherine Anne Porter's Near-Death Experience." *Anabiosis*, Fall, 1984, Vol. 4, pp. 107–123.

This paper contends that the main vision in Katherine Anne Porter's 1938 story "Pale Horse, Pale Rider," based on her nearly fatal bout with influenza during the epidemic of 1918, is a deep near-death experience of the type first described by Raymond Moody. Biographical sources and interviews with Porter are used to demonstrate the vision in the story and the physical and psychological effects the experience had on her. The story's vision of paradise is analyzed as an NDE. Two critical studies of the story are briefly discussed.

Rogo, Scott, "NDEs and Archetypes: Reply." *Anabiosis*, Fall, 1984, Vol. 4, p. 180.

Bibliography

This paper replies to the comments of Michael Grosso that the Scott Rogo in his paper on ketamine near-death experiences did not pay sufficient attention to Grosso's theory of archetypes in NDEs. Rogo clarifies his position on the archetype theory as a "nontheory" and contends that the pros and cons outlined for each of three ketamine NDE theories were presented from an objective, not personal, viewpoint. Although Rogo is favorably disposed to the idea of archetypes, no hard evidence that they exist has been evidenced in objective research.

Grosso, Michael, "NDEs and Archetypes." *Anabiosis*, Fall, 1984, Vol. 4, pp. 178–179.

Grosso offers an interpretation of near-death experience that uses the concept of archetypes. D. S. Rogo contended that this theory is a "nontheory" since it explains one unknown by another. Grosso claims that Rogo dismissed this theory too hastily, particularly in view of the fact that Rogo himself used the theory of archetypes to account for unusual apparitional experiences.

Siegel, Ronald, and Hirschman, Ada, "Hashish Near-Death Experiences." *Anabiosis*, Spring, 1984, Vol. 4, pp. 69–86.

This article reviews historical literature on hashish-induced near-death experiences. Most research endorsed the view of French psychiatrist Jacques Joseph Moreau that these experiences were hallucinations; others believed that hashish NDEs revealed an underlying reality as described in the works of Emanuel Swendenborg. Most accounts of these experiences resulting from high drug dosages contained elements and sequences of nondrug NDEs.